MW00630391

THE HEART HAS TO
ACHE

BEFORE IT LEARNS TO
BEAT

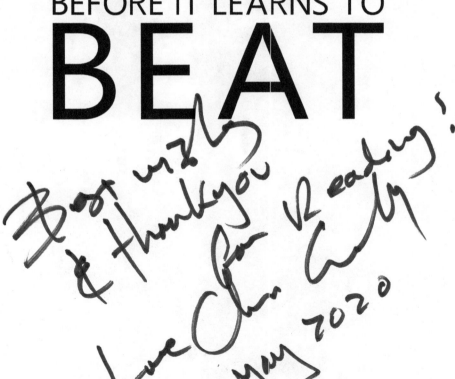

Best wishes
& Thankyou
for reading!
Love Clara Cutlry
May 2020

THE HEART HAS TO
ACHE
BEFORE IT LEARNS TO
BEAT

THE LYRICS & POEMS OF
CHRIS CONNELLY

SHIPWRECKED INDUSTRIES

Published by Shipwrecked Industries
November 2019
FIRST EDITION

DEDICATION

To Francesca Sundsten

CONTENTS

SOLO

SPECIAL PROJECTS

BANDS

FINI TRIBE

COLLABORATIONS AND UNUSED LYRICS

THE STRIP CLUB

FOREWORD

In the interests of full disclosure, Chris Connelly and I both hail
from Edinburgh, Scotland. As unlikely as it sounds, we first met in
the early to mid 80s whilst modelling in a show for local fashion
designers at the Edinburgh School of Art. We bonded over a mutual
amusement at being considered attractive enough for someone to
want us to model their clothes for them in public. We were often
to be found bent double in fits of hysterical laughter at catwalk
rehearsals as the choreographer shouted at us both to smile more.
This experience resulted in us becoming fast friends forever until
Chris left for America and his now legendary stints with The
Revolting Cocks and Ministry.

We had much in common. Both of us were in relatively successful
local bands. Both of us were singers. Both of us were obsessed with
Billy Mackenzie of iconic Scottish band The Associates. We both
loved to smoke and we were both at the time, committed cat people.

Chris was a prolific writer even back then. He was always scribbling
ideas in his notebooks, gifting particular poems or songs as surprise
birthday or Christmas gifts.

Writing was just something he did. All the time.

Nearly 35 years have passed since Chris and I tried to make it as
musicians back in Scotland. He has been constantly recording,
performing and writing all of this time which leads us to this
particular collection.

Sometimes bawdy and gaudy, sometimes deeply personal and often
unorthodox. No matter what he writes, he means it and it's always
intriguing. Beautiful even when occasionally opaque.

In this extensive collection of work dating as far back to 1980, some pieces which have never before been published until now, you will find it all. Poems, song lyrics, fragments. They are all held together here for the first time in one place.

This is your opportunity to get to know Christopher Connelly as I know him.

Iconoclast, Rockstar, Prophet. Father, friend, fine Bowie Impressionist and chimeric poet.

Shirley Manson

SOLO

WHIPLASH BOYCHILD

Daredevil

The bitter-edged distress
distempers parody,
move your burlesque
bite the heat eternity,
in half the time you'll dive
below your deficit,
and cut from top to bottom
we are the same.

Sink for a season,
returning to drown,
you will lift up a head for hex
to send the spirit down,
cold on the inside,
despite in your face,
the chain of disdain is unbroken,
dissolve,
and you leave no trace.

You freeze frame fanatic,
deliverance dies,
if the war be absurd,
then everything touched
will be your disguise.

Ghost of a Saint

Life out of breath,
living out the filth I have to face,
a loveless grin,

and the sweetest taste,

The distance is drained,
to where our lowly necks meet,
the urge is impassive,
as shadows lay framed in the heat,

And cold is the martyr,
his broken face melts in the rain,
proclaimed in procession,
of paradise wasted in pain…

The wounded surround us,
decayed in the ghost of a saint,
and cheated from rebirth,
eyes closed—and the heart becomes faint,
I start for a moment,
to count out the beasts I betrayed,
a need for the marvelous,
dies scorched,
in the bed where we laid.

This Edge of Midnight

The open machine wounds
unconscious diameter's drained,
the murder eclipsed by a moment of truth
for a fragment of pain,
flamed ground! The middle is distanced
and forged out of faith,
the same sound that touched us before
is now stained in its grave.

Into the middle
of an unexpected suicide at dawn,

your last admission of a brittle heat momentum
balanced—then it's gone.

Miracle madness retrieves
all that overrides trust,
full-scale fraternities modeled their debts
on a blood lust.
And your swansong unfolded betrayal
to send up in secret sight
go to the grace all that penetrates
this edge of midnight.

Cut that last chord.

Deserters in dragnets, the reign of reformers
all stabbed out of dreams,
you walk with the wane of the moon
where the cavalcade ended its means,
night speaks! Its ankle-deep destiny aimed at the moon,
Night speaks! To curse out the infidels burning up runes.

Damage deranged in the recoil
makes human face injuries,
the image of manhunt is clawed out of reach
with new sanities,
force fed perfection breeds two times the hate
for the beasts of the earth,
freeze out your fantasies blamed for the sake
of a rebirth.

Cut that last chord.

A blackout circumference is aimed
at an age without circumstance solved.
Icons conceived of a deadlock decision to breathe,

Sun-damaged rooms levitate in an era of secrets involved,
acrobat care/worms are stunted, preparing to leave.
Then leave us now!
While volumes are open, and shut out the heat.

The heat of heart murmur
controls the distortion of wake,
cascade in your limits,
confession's arrival of hate,
without light: the waking is gentle as thirst disappears,
without light: your speaking evasion remembered in tears,

Cut that last chord.

The Last of Joy

The stars are always there,
and praying towards the shoreline,
collapsed into the crests,
where drowning is the best,

Join hands as we walk to the water,
our lights turned out for a while,
sucked in by sinking sand,
I must let go your hand.

Don't look down.

Stowaway

The sound of secrets,
in faith falling,
steer demented, uninvited driving game,
here falls the bloodshed blame…

Stowaways contort the air,
your arms revolving in clockface stare,
bite the fossil,
framed against your Fahrenheits.

You've been smoked out
with a strange surprise—
cold, unfractured against your lies,
shattered-head bridges are underhand,
destroying asylums on the sand.

You want to be alive
when it happens,
blind exits fly,
when the voices cry,
abrupted again for a dream in a second,

What little is known
of the current intact—
a resurrection under glass,
your skin begins,
the hours are hours inside,
a dream in a second
or warped against the night.

The Hawk, the Butcher, the Killer of Beauties

If you were praying for an early eclipse,
to fold the greed within the spectrum shift,
the gaping misfortune in the drain of disdain,
white out the night if we reach home again.

The hawker indicates magnificate fear,
too cold for comfort in this hatemosphere,

I knelt down beside her melting heart and hell,
too drunken to see where her faithlessness fell.

The mixed in beliefs again,
betrayal in heat again,
a need to release in the comfort
of sideway shadows—
all playing at cutting the creeps in two.

She is only the tenth to remind me,
a deafening slant on the desperate man,
carousel movements in anti-terrain
blow holes between the legs of her shame.

The murderer passed as a magus,
hiding for fear that his guilt disappears,
alone is the butcher in surrogate stains
breaking his back to reach home again.

The Game is All Yours

I crossed the line
where shadows followed
the black sand signs
to realize,
what indiscretion
will carry me on home
tonight?

The fear of waking divides the sun,
to underneaths and overreach,
what liquid light
will carry me alone
tonight?

Where liars crawl,
and murder rests again,
hold up in secrets
forever and ever.
'Till we pass over again,
in quarters, never replicas,
the undivided
folds, and folds again
in fleshwounds
tearing out the heart of fright,
never ending for the heart of fright.

Well you're trapped
between your rising sign,
and downward spirals
never shine,
outside glass angled targets
seem to move with fright,
where rooftop snipers
aim and fire to
cut the night.

Confessions of the Highest Bidder

The blood of our horizons,
the weeping sores of the sun,
wax and wane,
the uncertainty of four cornered fathoms,
oft' frayed—a realization,
of fear born,
of infertility,
thriving on fright,
in the chopping block night.

The shadow is your father,

in a hunting gown hides…
the pain is your mother
in burial mode…
her body is writhing
from the sons
she shall not bare.

If only the darkest of the gems
would not sting her,
as she runs away barefoot
from the hunter,
and if only it were not me
who solemnly sacrificed
the jewels she had left
for second best.

The gems begin to move in this night war;
halfway between crystal and insect,
her sting is more venomous
than the afterbirth ache
which is constantly around me.
I am the only awareness
in this hellhole,
and filled so full of contradictions
that I will never walk in a straight line again,

My mother is rotting,
and I would see her dead,
her pale blue skin like cold, cold rubber
decorating dead branches
where leaves used to grow.

The night burns awake
from the afterbirth ache.

PHENOBARB BAMBALAM

July

It was raining on love from within my room
and the walls began to warp,
the colours of my things were all washed out and wrong,
and the lights began to short,
I heard you call out my name,
but I couldn't find the way, and the floors were too steep,
then your face in the light,
became the shadow of fright,
it killed you to sleep.

There was just enough light for me to watch you leave
through a hole in the wall,
should I build or burn your effigy
while the buildings fall?
I refuse to become a martyr,
no matter what you say,
I'll be gone this time tomorrow,
I only live for today.

I moved the figure of your past in hiding
into the street,
you were cold and grey, decaying,
and you couldn't even speak,
I pulled out the sins from my mouth of disease
and I begged for the truth,
I was cursed by way of comparison,
it broke me in two.

I spat upon my unmarked grave
in the heat of the spite,

I screamed my insect litanies in the middle of the night,
"Bury the martyr to his neck and feed him to the worms!"
Replace his blood with toxins,
look at him burn!

God, I hate July,
I screamed up to the sky,
for what it's worth,
on the face of this earth,
I refuse to be denied.

Come Down Here

Beyond the soft, wet silence,
shadow's midnight mind.
The warmth appeared in seconds,
like the dark.
A trail of swollen fruit
leads to a higher kind,
lips and lovers' limbs
begin to part.

Search, and you shall find,
what you want,
take what's mine,
breathe, in the air,
of the hour
we were there.

In the middle of the magic
is a perfect flower,
in the heat of the moment
is a flame,
it all comes from you to me
to you

in a secret shower,
and blends the blood inside
'till we're the same.

I disappeared between you many times before
and every single time
I never leave,
awake with you and stranded
on another shore,
too dreamlike and delirious
to believe.

Bring in the night,
and the moon,
and the light,
shake off the day
you were born
and we'll stay.

Close to the skin,
shut your eyes,
we begin,
fall, like a leaf,
onto me
in your sleep.

Too Good to Be True

The moment explodes every evening,
a fountain of flames melts the way,
here she comes now collecting predictions,
a waking eclipse with nothing to say.

A paper-thin prayer will herald the morning,
sent up in a scare you held in your sleep,

it burnt in the sun before we could see it,
a waking emission that no one could keep.

Past came to life,
flew away and died,
makes you wonder why
that's in a daydream
fell to the ground,
made an empty sound
dead to the world,
came back to me,

Too good to be true...

I tried to make sense of seclusion,
a million to one in the rain,
a thorn in the side of my sanity
silenced the background of disdain,

Who in the world will comfort disaster?
what in the world will save me tonight?
look at the stains that cover the ocean,
look at the daydreams burning in flight,

Say it isn't true,
what I said to you,
I could never breathe,
for fear of waking,
look at the signs,
every one of mine,
never any time
waiting for me,

Too good to be true...

Heartburn

I stare from behind the mirror,
I still can't feel a thing,
this house has been dead for years,
it doesn't mean anything,
the walls all soaked with indifference,
the rooms occupied with despair,
the bed rots in its own ignorance,
the windows just open and stare.

The climate of unhappy families,
all covered with dirt and with flies,
breeding a hole for our secrets,
so we can watch them all grow into lies,
at the same time the rooms seem to mock you,
parading your shadow of doubt,
they pray for our silent audience,
and beg for forgiveness without...

I dreamed for years before now,
I'd end up in a place like this,
too scared in a room I refuse to call home,
I knew it would end like this,
I walk with the weight on my shoulders,
of the promises that I broke,
to get rid of these filthy secrets,
and throw them down that same hole.
This house is a house of failure,
of bitterness and remorse,
of illness, betrayal, and torture,
it means nothing, of course,
in the corner, I swear I can hear,
the ghost of you screaming at me,
questioning misplaced virtues,

and my infidelity.

And even though I did not doubt you,
no one said that you had to be right,
the light and the air that surround me,
couldn't turn my day into night,
the company of the corpse here beside me,
will haunt me forever like your screams,
like everything else never leaves me alone,
from my waking hours into my dreams.

No Lesser of Two Evils

"It's the changing face of sanctuary"
she told me to my face,
far beyond the code of innocence,
you're eager to replace,
I retorted with the reasoning,
she may be hypnotized,
with a closely guarded secret,
then I looked into her eyes,

"Give me one good reason"
and the reasoning's gone,
take apart your solitude,
and tell me I'm wrong,
Rome's still burning
in my dreams every night,
sordid and serious,
she turned out the light,

What was mine crumbled,
and she walked outside.
it was the last time
I saw her alive,

In the face of deception,
and the virtues involved,
I can't say that I was surprised…

Ambition grabbed me tenderly
like lovers to the end,
security and purity,
my two and only friends,
I could walk into disaster,
she could jump into a lake,
then I realized the obvious
was all we had to state;

"If you can't see me,
then I can see through myself"
She alone is careless
'till she breathes someone else,
"What's in between us?
Is it ghost? Is it greed?"
A well-defined prediction
of the life that we lead…

Maybe I should turn around,
because I'm lying to myself,
address, caress me,
no, don't!
I believe I'm someone else…

Ignition Times Four

What you bring upon yourself,
today of all days,
you need help,
mind collapsing/middle anguish
cure of folly, in the dark

today of all days,
twilight seemed so desperate,
adjacent to your crime,
ignition escalates:

Times one,
Times two,
Times three,
Times four.

You wouldn't know it,
but the kid was right,
moving sideways in a sun dance
to avoid the light:

Depth and true distance,
Depth and true distance,
Depth and true distance,
Depth and true distance,

Times one,
Times two,
Times three,
Times four.

Dirtbox Tennessee

Standing at the crossroads pouring salt in his wounds,
corroded wasted alcohol erection afternoon,
before the eyes of whisky caught out right by the sun,
I'd never try to hurt you
'cos I love everyone
now I pull my way with snakes baked hard in the heat,
dead birds and putrid human trash and ulcerated meat,
across the way a blind man but he don't remember me,

how I tore apart a happy home
down in dirtbox Tennessee.

And I can hear the birds and babies squawkin',
cryin' to their moms,
they're askin' where their daddy's gone
and why he's been so long,
but they don't know he's lyin' down with his hands between his
     thighs
to resurrect the impotent worm before he dies,
you can push and pull all you want
but you can't raise the dead,
you can lie on your back and choke on soil
while the insects give you head.

And now the blind guy and his halfwit son
are gonna roll me for my drink,
sucking me up through gap-toothed grins
and spitting out a jinx,
the high priest of halitosis
and his inbred ugly kid
whose name is Elvis Aaron afterbirth
and I'll kill him for what he did,
he pulled down my bloodstained pants
and he forced apart my legs,
his dad said "shoot your best shot kid"
and he shot until I bled.

And now the blood, mixed with glass,
mixed with come, mixed with all the afternoon sun,
praise the lord and pass the gun,
a crucifix in a rented room
that sticky night with a burning moon,
she swore to god I would see her dead
on the night of the day that we were wed,

it's all for love, precious love,
lie down dear while I disappear,
this crock of shit
and a belly full of rancid beer,
I do it for you, only you…

SHIPWRECK

Candyman Collapse

In some kind of certain,
the treasure does wait,
I walk with a yardstick,
and I hesitate,
it's some kind of virtue,
painting "love me" on the walls
broken comfort mends an atmosphere
of pressure that falls into hands that steal,
don't you know a false ideal,
is best when you don't reveal…

Goodbye my baby,
it's time that I should go,
just why I don't remember—
but I love you so,
an alarming force of nature,
the gods don't understand,
sends me reeling for redemption
and a show of hands me back
to the time I dared,
rather than the time I cared,
now I always wake up scared…

I should grow and I should learn,
what to build and what to burn,
I've got nothing left to say,
in my favour I've got you,
if there's nothing left to prove,
at least I've been king for a day…

Spoonfed Celeste

Take me back to that Sunday afternoon,
a baptism, a sermon, and Celeste with a spoon,
she told me that the choir was unrehearsed,
they prick themselves with needles,
the altar boys perverse!
What's in a family?
Keep it in the family!
Salivating eyes,
ready to make a meal of me!

Uncle Tom informs me
he's too scared to disrobe,
a Catholic maybe, a drunk one certainly,
Paul and Mhairi rendering my baby-toys destroyed,
Celeste looking daggers
at the congregation's joy.
Here comes my family!
God forbid the family!
They haunt me with their eyes.

Force fed with spoon,
she came too soon—poor Celeste.

And reaching up to choke the whiskey priest,
the makings of a funeral
where no one is deceased,
Celeste, she could contain herself no more,
she stole me from my uncle's arms
and headed for the door,
looking down she said to me,
welcome to the family,
the hunger in her eyes!
Wanting to make a meal of me.

The congregation passed me in a line,
and opted for the alcoholic priest to pour the wine,
it seemed to me Celeste was trying to hide,
a sanctus, then a litany,
then back into the night,
I'm not your mummy,
this is not your family,
it hurt to have to lie.

Force fed with spoon,
she came too soon—poor Celeste.

What's Left but Solid Gold?

I gave you precious metal,
my precious metal friend,
to cast a spell for famine,
you kept it in your hand,
I'm loathe to strike a bargain
to auction off my past,
for purpose-built protection,
where gold looked down and laughed.

What stain on a bad name?
Clawing the wings off a fly,
sowing disease in a harvest,
infants pretending to die.

The strong invented solace,
to comfort us with rage,
and bleed on constellations,
strung neatly in my cage,
What's left but solace starving?
What's left but solid gold?
The edge of light in hiding,

the last of night controlled.

Pests bite 'til they're frantic,
spitting through peepholes at me,
salivate, sanguine intention,
hacking through veins to be free.

Both hands to betrayal,
mine became the first,
alchemist to ice age,
precious metal curse.

Precious,
precious,
precious,

So down they came in secret,
stars on separate shores,
their likeness cast in mantras,
immortalized with ores,
if alchemy is sacred—
metallurgy is waste,
it leaves behind a scar,
on your
precious metal face…

Detestimony III

Do you remember me
from when the curse became my eyes?
I could walk through a space
that could lose my face,
many lifetimes in disguise,
throw on the blackest robes,
and steal from your brother's wake,

redefine yourself as pity,
born once again too late.
I can't stop the rain from calling
men to fire off waste,
spent a year in the place
with an enemy
only faith will see our limbs burn,

Strangers came and comfort left,
we questioned those who questioned death,
the more we gave away,
the more they grew,
nations turned their heads from light,
rejoiced like only darkness might,
and burst through faded walls
that we once knew.

Six signs in front of me
melt back towards the sun,
another freezing day to welcome you,
you've been gone too long my son,
we traded energy
like we still had a lot to spare,
of course the end result was deliberate,
and the benefits were rare,
I can't stop this will from breaking,
the isolated stares,
will reduce me to that of a criminal,
and the faith that is left now,
swords controlled by unknown souls,
break habits by reversing roles,
the mind completes the cycle
then you die,
filled our drinking cups with dust,
coated weapons red with rust,

and pissed on naked people
from the sky.

Anyone's Mistake

The rain drove him outside,
a shadow intact
as he crawls down the pavement
too drunk and oblivious
to tell which is moon and is mine
he's scared of himself,
you can tell by the weight of the waves
in his bloodstream,
delinquently soaking him,
leaving a shine,

Beneath his feet the bottle makes peace,
gently it rolls into nothing
he cries, but the wind caught his breath
and the night never heard him scream
stay.
Won't you fold your secrets away,
to a calm place where secrets can lie.

The truth beyond stars
drove a hole through his daydreams
it made him think twice about
lines between fantasy
getting a grip on the past,
the perfect dilemma
is starting to fight
in the bottle tonight,
it chokes like a genie,
coughs up three wishes
and shatters the glass.

The neck is broken,
the liquid appears,
gently intoxicates back to the womb,
but he don't want to go there
he'll stay in his room
and sing stay…

Drench

I heard a shot from the outside,
I heard a shot from between,
unloading fever for favour,
I don't know where to begin,
fadeout burnt into silver,
I could have lived without sin,
disguised as angels on church walls,
I don't know where to begin.

I stole the gifts I wanted to,
destroyed them, gave them back to you,
a famous blank on a famous page,
the story burned itself with age.

Discount the snipers as brainwashed,
persuade your leaders to hide,
closed circuit damaged in sacrifice,
wait for the drench to decide,
in stations, gravity's sacred,
the slogan covered the floor,
unseen by passengers riding,
obscured by snipers before.

I stole the gifts I wanted to,
destroyed them, gave them back to you,
a famous blank on a famous page,

the story burned itself with age.

The Early Nighters
(for River Phoenix)

The skylit grey parade,
she always said,
look for the future
in a missing beat instead,

No questions asked of you,
but rumour has spoke,
disguising the fault lines
in the miracle of smoke,

Why pay the price
of an early night?

Reaching out for comfort
and finding a curse,
you could do worse…
celebrating the moment
that poisons your hand,
try to understand, they grow,
the early nighters
stop the flow
and die young.

In dream-like ports of call
setting hope to sail,
shipwrecked by your own mistakes
the sirens start to wail,
the merging of spirits walk,
and their hands are joined,
cascades to a resting place

their faces light with joy

Why pay the price
of an early night?

With the splendour of silence
you gracefully fall—
nowhere at all
you decided to tell me with warmth in your voice
try to understand,
they grow,
the early nighters
stop the flow
and die young.

Swimming

I went to the river to ease my pain,
I'm feeling so tidal that I'm starting to wane,
decided to set one foot in the flow,
then up to my knees and in the water I go…

It's messing around with the rate of my heart,
feels like I'm in love and the water's so dark,
I wonder if she's here to hold my hand?
To rescue what's left of the drowning man,

Learning to swim on my own…

Well is it just icy or a fit of remorse?
My legs are so heavy and my lungs start to burst,
now which is the water and which one is me,
locating the places that I want to be…

I never expected such an easy release,

traumatically downstream and now I'm at peace,
clutching at pebbles on the bank of my tomb,
still learning to swim I think it's safe to assume.

Model Murmur

Cold out a maze,
a maze became
no half-beast forthcoming
no, not you again,
lips hung below
a Midas touch
swing low, lips so sweetly ache
the two of us

Oh no, not you again,
oh no, not you again,
oh no, not you again,
oh…

Off current rules,
in cardiacs,
dream back new surroundings,
fight off party acts,
a gleam expires,
you rented death
oblique spawns chaos
only seconds left

Oh no, not you again,
oh no, not you again,
oh no, not you again,
oh…

The silence fits

right over it,
bring your hand down hard,
and suffer it,
a broken right
to finish all,
bring your hand…

Meridian Afterburn

The old west shines demise
on prairies' good-byes,
levitates the twilight sand,
won't clean my hand,
what we've become—
a sunset gun,
pours beast abroad to harbour god.

What desert crimes
steamed awake into the magus,
blank dreams on horseback
delivered here to save us,
crossed paths where cattle grind
with skeletons and herders,
all in the borrowed sun.

Last praying thunderheads
shine fire on less grace,
unbranded werewolves dream in pain,
in scattered bells,
and shattered spells,
arachnids fled the watershed.

Our volunteers flayed alive
by war of virtue
slurred speech predicts

the damaged half
that wants to hurt you,

Head west in fruitless search
of wind that carries prayer,
all in the borrowed sun.

Constellated like birds into breathless,
broken names are buried here,
sandstreams that the elders have left us,
load their banks and disappear,
cry, sinking like fractured jaws to the north.

Torrential flies to meet you
under burnt bridge,
brings back the fore noon to our own,
great static plains
and timeless rains
leaves afterburn,
then we adjourn.

Shipwreck

I hope no one can find me
recessed in these waves quite alone,
although grounded inside me,
the fever bleached out by the sun,
are you gonna gauge your rage by the stars?
Lift me on your shoulders to see where we are?
Every ripple brings a gift to your feet,
some of them worthless,
some of them sweet,

I'm as soaking wet as your eyes,
grey robs blue

and heads for the skies,
here comes another shipwreck
to pass in the night
design your own sunset and drop out of sight.

You give to me what splendour is left submerged
oh baby, don't worry, I'll drown enough for two,
it's sinking, believe in it,
I'll stay with my ship and ask;
oh, kiss me Hardy, the albatross
Columbus and Drake,
oh baby, don't worry,
you won't feel a thing,
it's cold and it's simple,
but it's the only way I know to breathe free…

It was proven in darkness,
the drugs and the water mix well,
if I come across heartless,
I lost what I knew when I fell,
in a pool of light you rescue your wings,
try to fly away from desperate things,
every piece of fortune is lost for today,
I won't hold my breath
as it sweeps me away,
here it comes…

THE ULTIMATE SEASIDE COMPANION

Mississippi Palisades

Mississippi, close your eyes
and be safe, the only fire tonight
is candlelight,
and it sure feels right.
I can all but drink you from the palisades,
I can stare the living banks outright
'cos I live outside,
and it sure feels right.

I've been sent here
to find the truth
of an underwater dialogue
I shared with you,
I was several thousand years
in making sense of you.

Maybe your own princess's temper
burst in clouds
to get away from you,
unload the boats
you should be working
on a night like this,
I beg of you.

Mississippi, you fell over yourself,
to the caves of South Dakota
I say we do retreat,
doesn't that sound neat?

My East is Your West

You work through times of change,
amongst other things,
you're more than adept
and though this time it's strange,
I will visit you,
my east is your west,

Did I hear you
through the bells Saint Peter had to offer?
Did they lose you, and find your faith
now you can pray forever.

Inside a priestly nod,
amongst other things,
your angels escape
and now your secret's out,
with a knowing wink,
your faith is disgraced,

All these angels,
with bits of you
you did not want to offer,
are ascending,
but you're too heavy,
guilt descends forever,

When you open your eyes to me.

I bet on horses that our secret side
would rid us of saints,
create a space for shame,
we will feed off it
'til our voices are faint.

Did I hear you
through the bells Saint Peter had to offer?
Did they lose you, and find your faith
now you can pray forever.

Stray

A missing knock will leave you stray,
unheard of flight and the hands go back.
To try and make the sound go away,
crippled tick-tock,
in a city built on fleeing disgrace.

What will the north bring you next?
All subjects you breathe on
you cannot buy.

Empty Sam

It's darkest in the morning
light dropping down in poles,
shards metal evening
when dawn gets too close,

A dog bites its owner
to remind him of his pain,
father's dragged by horses
to remind him why he came,

I cut down all my friends
to see where I might lie,
on simple blades of unlit truth
the truth will bleed you dry,

Don't dream no eyeless dream

'cos you might wake up blind,
your hands around a stranger's throat
reborn the killing kind,

From wicked blue there hangs a rock
to make your god stand straight,
you find you can't rebuild your world
collapsing from its weight.

No More Changing of the Guard

No more
no more waiting here alone
the victims come and go
far beyond
what they wrote
literate,
or simply good for a quote

Alas
all that ends well starts to spoil
it lives just to deceive us
for a while
we would shine, in our way
decay is love out of time

So much for waiting here
nothing ever came
it simply wasted us, here

Sometimes
all the risks you took declined
the other invitations
to collapse
or just die

innocent:
oh, stay alive for a while

No more
no more changing of the guard
the guard that never changes
leaves you last
or not at all
celebrate
the wait is good for you all.

Island Head

We crawled like sea dogs to the shore
the blades of wind blew back
the sand we knew before
when we are tired it's pointless trying to move ahead
just let the shanty breathe you
or we could just float for miles
before the surface breaks you
or the ground escapes you
you're a many acted play
you're chaos
swimming back a mile or two
to island head

In your eyes there happened age that clung to winter
like a flock starved overseas
don't mean to be familiar, but you think a lot like me
and if the fancy takes us
we can feed the birds a crust
they will fly back to their nest eggs
they will cry for love

Oh begone their power of flight!

No singing,
just screaming 'til the land will end
oh island head.

Toledo Steel

The weight of this barge is heavy, so,
somehow I did know,
your cargo's blazing downstream,
I see it through the steam.
All the gulls that follow you,
their calls are dedications,
they are real.
Until that day you wonder what the hold contains,
we place our wages on Toledo steel.

Caravan

You might just remember
where you last were hiding out
where the grey-eyed ones they seek to be
oh my love, the heat was restless
we were too scared to leave the shade
but the flames were burning up the trees

Settle down, your temper shows, you know
it rains back on itself
like a storm spits in a mirror for relief
though both of us are followers
we can both move without our fingers pointing
slowly, to elation or to grief

Oh but testaments before us read of stranger things
we're farther than the caravan could reach
and I know the sand deserts us,

but the desert breaks us down
and its tale's too obsolete for him to reach

Forty days can soon become a multitude of things
a penance, plague, the mysteries in prayer
forty nights will see the last reversed
and turned into a freezing faith
and casting curses back into the air
you endear yourself to salt and sand
and iron rings surround you
like a railroad to redemption or to war
break that ring of deserts shattered
and the whole of love will burn with you
confront you with the world you're fighting for.

To Play a Slow Game

I'd like to play a slow game
will it fade?
Will it win me again?
Solace last
players jeopardized by games they passed
or ignored
don't even cross a game so slow
oh
it's time to play again
you should know

Through the air
only chaos is red
leave the age
but the cause is already dead
signatures
and the molding of cheats
sleight of hand

breathe down every street.

The Ultimate Seaside Companion

Darling, I must confess,
these moments of mine don't come easy,
darling, I told you more or less,
be sure as we drive to the sea
as sure as the evening that caves in on me
darling, take a look outside
these bells greet, the spirits fly, the moments rush,
the ice dies,
the sun greets, a sacrifice to us.

More, I just cannot say:
drive the car into the waves,
love grew in stranger ways
like the sea that fell from grace.

Darling, if you could see me now,
the last of my blues lost at sea,
darling, if you believe me now,
be sure sound the horn for these souls,
be sure say a prayer when the island bell tolls,

Darling, build your oceans wide,
your castles, asylums, are sand on the island
the grappling hook the driftwood now float free.

The Fortune II

Where are the masks that prepared us for winter?
Where are the fields where we moved from the centre?
The last pulse of moon,
revolves by a question, it's timeless, rewarded

by lesser suggestion.

Grow past a fortune, it forges your sign,
tools we would use for bringing back time,

Sane—it would bleed into visions of those
blame studies skin like its eyes never closed,
the eyes never closed, we missed a fortune.

Fate like the arms crossed
with staggering truths
shock wakes our grasps,
when all mysteries proved,
Matches in marvel, the season we wait
when curse turns to care,
our minds were too late…

The last pulse of moon
revolves by a question,
it's timeless, rewarded
by lesser suggestion.

Chorus of Eyes

I live for the day your deliberate eyes look over my way,
birds never so high as they flew to the sun because they can't wait,
we follow them up,
we find we can't stop.

I fight back the years that your memory stole,
your likeness in tears,
brave soldiers are we,
complicated or not
we fight and believe.

Consumed by an all-encompassing love of your eyes.
Caress of endless eyes,
chorus ends us, sighs,
blinking is nothing but blindness to me,
counting 'til you fall asleep.

I could write a book on the riches deserved by such sedative eyes,
the band in a chorus of envy declare that the sun's not that bright,
we shine 'til we sigh
a chorus of eyes.

Your look stares a path through the wilderness worn by the greyest
    of days,
and shot through with gold,
like your veins in the cold
the magic just stays.

Thunderland Reel

Oh, my love we partake of this reel,
all the children asleep and their faces upturned to the stars
and the sky is a diamond struck wheel,

And the fountain awakens,
baptizes with water,
the name of the god is unclear but you gotta kneel down.

You would move like a storm across the floor bringing light
to the blurred eyes of jealous bled lovers who quickly surround.

Oh my love the search did belong
to the price on the head of a ghost,
we've been searching too long
and the way we did search was all wrong,

And the birds swoop around this diamond struck wheel,
they are crying to heaven,
they move in the truest of reels.

And the saints are not sorry you came,
their conclusions dry faster than clay in the sun,
the most barren of fields.

BLONDE EXODUS

London Fields

In this city I dredge tonight,
will you come walk with me?
Tell everyone you know
you're movin' kind of slow
for a while…

I never met a shadow
that I didn't like,
I never was afraid to walk where there was no light,
never met a woman whose shadow and light
could prove my dear,
walkin' after midnight
only faith in my hands
can lose my fear.

A half-expected flash
within the distance
and we are alone,
oh, we could walk towards it
or ignore it,
try to find it on our way home,

There lies a point in time
when the sun won't shine,

I don't care about the sun anymore
when the dark is mine,
oh the dark is mine,
the dark is mine…

We jumped from roof
to scandalous rooftop pretending to fall,
we celebrated treasures of moonlight
in the gutters we crawled,
Seems the stars are perpetual scars on a blue skinned bird
flying low, ungodly creatures ask the people
of a sleepless world...

Diamonds Eat Diamonds
(For Billy Mackenzie)

Host devouring delight,
in the far cry of a city light,
most she gave back to me,
in the weak guise of a parasite,
falling she cried,
"Time is a wretched companion,"
its floating dominion,
sells itself short as a lullaby,
maybe tonight I don't feel as strong
as I felt on the floor,
but so long ago,
I should've just sat up
and settled the score.

Please come over,
money's the last thing I want,
if I could will you, sweet angel,
back to the front,
I would force my doors open,
kiss you like diamonds eat diamonds.

I saw your precious mania diving for pearls,
and swan dive like Icarus, into the underworld,
clutching at air to be born on the ground,

with a heartbeat like history
that never was found.
Flowing ice stallions too near to be back in my arms,
give me your millions,
I'll replace it with charm,
faith from the past,
reinvents all our lives,
a sick flick of the wrist,
marching companions,
disappearing like diamonds in mist.

Please come over,
money's the last thing I want
if I could will you sweet angel,
back to the from
I would force my doors open,
kiss you like diamonds eat diamonds.

What's that from?
It's that melody's broken song,
in my world, we've been mining for much too long,
in these eyes there are ghosts you will never meet,
kiss you like diamonds eat diamonds eat diamonds
eat diamonds eat diamonds eat diamonds eat
diamonds...

Blonde Exodus I

What we expect on a night like this,
all the peepholes in the world outgrew the sun,
all the telephones ring louder than creation,
and their numbers dialing back to less than one,
all numbers dialed without much sanity,
because the answers won't forth come.

Throw the towel in on the runway,
it's easiest to do,
because the audience think mostly,
you were told to,
a flashbulb for an echo,
well that bombshell didn't last,
in Vogue Italia there's a secret cast,
of new agendas we suggest,
she'd run a mile,
it's not her style.

Blonde exodus—they travel mostly late at night
in a reel beneath the bedsprings
all the stars could not contain
their maiden flight.

So tell me—how d'you get to make that trip?
from Chicago to Milano,
the engine spits out ashes
burned from torn men's lips.
Do you wanna dance?
Do you want to fill the room
with every empty room you ever knew?
Carousels define your hunger, child,
before the crowd you're dancing wild.

You say your world crash landed
in a blaze of magazines,
all open to where the page describes you best,
now Magdalene is burning,
your face in quarantine,
the safest place—my angel's mirrored walls,
undress, photographers will call,
she'd run a mile,
it's not her style.

Twilight Shiner

I meant to turn around,
too afraid to pick you up,
no flies on this boy,
come too soon, farthest afternoon,

Get set, we're freezing, falling angels
on a rooftop paradise,
no flies, her wings are torn and shapeless,
you twilight shiner, you
you'd leave us if you could.

Fly away, twilight shiner
remind me if it all goes well,
you throwaway, I just can't tell,
the farthest thing from my mind is tonight,
fly away, twilight shiner,
the fountainheads and corridors,
where we once laughed and fought our wars,
now echo like they took away the light.

Count all your blessings my fortunate son,
then expose them to the sun,
like some Greek fable, they'll wish you away,
just like twilight, return again next day.

Some bird reflected you in song,
and he told us you were wrong,
the pain that pushed us both apart,
just can't read a broken heart,
it's the strangest place to start.

Angels spill aftermath tonight,
we shall all turn our heads tonight.

Fly away…

Blue Hooray

I'm the temper that brought you December,
the ice of a lonely stray,
the map of the last time we met carved into your blue hooray,
if I become weary of sight in the instant your heart grows nails,
for a room that's inside, whose doors open wide
and the marriage has failed.
Though I can't dance,
can't I convince you to promenade?
A 4 AM blitz to the fountain of youth
is that all you have?
Absolute gentle that's here to remind you
the frames of an unseen film,
puts all your faith back and forth, every frame
like a colourless twenties still.

Candle lights overlooked your photographs,
adjoining madness in a burning book I wrote to last.

I'm the closest you'll get to collapsing,
the slave to a perfect day,
your lovers drop molten mistakes
burned into your blue hooray,
the cost of liaisons will far exceed pennies
exchanged for lust,
and the map of the last time we kissed
breathes it's last as it turns into dust,
you'll stand beneath all impermanence,
wait for the band to play,
you forge an alliance with fraudulence,
and a stolen bouquet.

You were always hoping that I'd
immortalize you in a song.

Magnificent Wing

I was walking on anger's
magnificent wing,
like beating black eyelids,
they're furious things,
and I moved through the distance
in a figure of eight,
and the beast might be landing,
but it's always too late,

I caressed the explosion
with the strength of a gun,
and the bullets will tell you,
there is always the sun,
when love is delivered,
in a weight round your neck,
she is here to move slowly,
she is here to protect,

Damn those angels, send them up to me,
cast that stone in heavens wake
and leave us on our own,
I beg you to sing magnificent wing.

The ascent drove a message
back home to your grave,
in the desert surrounding,
we will never be saved,
great journeys avoid us,
like criminals lie,
and the people we trusted

are waving goodbye.

We'll build from the ashes
of Saint Christopher's town,
and as soon as we are finished,
we will burn it back down,
and the rains they won't help us,
they'll distort what we wrote,
and we'll drink from the deluge
where the idiots float.

The Long Weekend

Another Saturday night,
all mid-America's hands outstretched
back to that Saint Louis light,
all hands upon the bridge,
she's trying to make out cries and sighs
to reach out
to where her loved ones live,

Thought about a dream I had
down in southern Illinois,
Sam Shepard was there
looking for a place to die.

Follow a path,
but you will always fall into
the scream, the dream
that's falling into you,
oh, misty motions!
Drink yourself into a dare,
I promise you
the river doesn't care,

Try to steal what the west will never give
on cry-baby bridge
we're both here,
but the two of us can't live
on cry-baby bridge.

The railroad journey's end,
the rust belt drags its weary soul
and buries it near Baltimore,
we're standing on the bridge
and looking at the train's eclipse
it shines to where the valley slips.

Sailing on a plain
is the ghost of the terrain
you can almost see it fade
into the timeless ocean of the Everglades.

Drink your fill,
because the bridge it never will,
she'll drink the river dry before her legend dies
secure your place upon the bridge, a last embrace
before your brilliant horses try to race.

Julie Delpy

In the farthest thing resolved in your life,
the happy sad side of an earthquake,
seen in heavenly light,
rest your head against the mountain as it falls,
amused, a rag and bone reflection come alive…

When you wake, a voice on the radio
pleads you to resist,
all coming of age, or quote unquote rage,

or calculated risk,
who's the fool who told you love is still for sale?
Amusing, and your heart's still beating back in time...

When you walk, everything will stop
and I want you, most sincerely, to acknowledge pride of place,
when all your life appears to be a waste...

When Julie calls, you ate all your ice cream,
and hearts refuse to beat,
and flavour, a contemptuous slave,
to the friends you want to meet,
throw yourself into the friction left downtown,
a drink, a dance, a bet on the horses,
come around...

A crime dissolves and turns into virtue,
only in your mind,
and my resolve, returning to flirt with you,
by your heart's design,
break the marvelous dark that throws you to yourself,
and reads aloud, redundant accounts, from a life...

When you walk, everything will stop
and I want you most sincerely, to acknowledge pride of place,
when all your life appears to be a waste...

Blonde Exodus II

Her past, a walkway into private rooms,
her means a sheet on ashen floors,
afraid the fountain that will cleanse her,
reveals her naked, unadored,
I sincerely apologize,
stinging eyes, velvet smoke,

let's see what the opposite can be,
her life story dressed in quotes.

And the furthest thing you'll find in that room,
is the hardest thing to do,
why'd she laugh? It's not that funny,
safe and shaking back to you.

Unveil the prophets with a price to pay,
all faded masks with no front teeth,
a climbing vine that chokes hysteria,
betrays the issue of her grief,
girl, I gave immortality,
it's the least I could do,
backfired, you are permanently tired,
until I take it back from you.

Silver shadows on her breasts appear,
and they tear apart the room,
sordid gestures born of mourning,
broken promises too soon.

Freeze those shadows as your finest hour,
you'll remember them in time,
rewrite your memoirs like you've lost all power,
on your door, replace the sign.

I was walking with some nameless rage,
my heart a quickly blazing hole,
you said you thought that you could never age,
without the passage of control.

PRIVATE EDUCATION

Harbour Days

There's blood on the sand
where I put my own hand
there's a motion of milestones too far,
she is staring me down
in the harbour we found,
it was harder to find in the dark,
not by sweeping green lamplight,
or sweeping green eyes,
by the bleed me clean dice they decide.

Outside of my lodgings,
through the crossfire of seagulls,
through the sword fighting masts
and the suicide rockpools,
she did walk like a child,
head down, feet in the water
dragging in brine,
counting back time.

Hallelujah, here comes harbour days,
and tide worth wading back to you,
though I'll miss you between the rocks,
we must go our separate ways,
take the tide back to harbour days.

She's a cut lip to citrus,
through the waterwing cries
of the birds feeding frenzy,
and a path is cut dry,
cast a net over wishes,

and I draw back but starfish,
just a landed reflection
of heaven too soon,
cast a net over shadows,
by the act of her shyness,
and I draw back real beauty
but she just swims away.

There's a crisscross horizon
built of hieroglyph arrows
all pointing with weightlessness
hands to the stars,
all mayhem retained
in a cup drained by baby
she'll have peace to push forward
if she puts down the blade.

While arches increase
under bridges of grief,
all the water that goes
back to harbour day flows,
she will mistreat her motion
and that cripples my heart
she is breathless and frozen
as she drifts through the arch.

She is forced to obtain
patterned waves that contain
dead—of-winter-stone, iron clad
decisions of grandeur,
swing softly, I love you,
swing soft in the water,
though I'll never touch you
and it kills me to say
I love you

I love you.

Samaratin

Though the east was hard enough to beat,
so wicked in its heyday,
driving rivers to retreat,
over solace, we are a raincloud,
to drop dead ravens at your feet,
the rest were good at landing,
but not good enough to cheat.

A crisis of pale wisdom,
blanks the eyes and points the way,
to the misfires in the distance,
and the fractures of the day,
unrewarded, we bring havoc,
with our bonfires and our guns,
closely guarded—we're a stranglehold
and no two wars are won.

And be still, and be steel,
and we'll steal it back tonight.

Throwing blades
at unrecurring esplanades,
where the angles slide,
when they cut within you,
the farthest place to be is still outside.

Glass bleaker
than the AM hiss our radios emit,
mud scraped by our initials,
we have made a shallow pit,
serenade outclassed disciples,

tired of worshipping a hole,
neglected while your favourite game
is hoisted up a pole,

Did someone shape your world?
Who's knocking?
Isn't spite distilled?
Is it like this in your world?
Isn't like this in your world.
Too bad, stopping in your world.

You Versus Miracle

I can't believe before this miracle
motion to silence, before this twist of the arm,
or a lethal injection of sweetness and charm,
I was alright before contessa revealed
how contagious concealed
in a leather-bled diary
all lipstick inside
but she'll never step forward tonight.

Miracle versus the truth,
open Stanley knife blades,
and a version of you,
and the blood count is perfect,
it cuts you to shreds,
I wish I was the victim instead.

I can't believe that choking on laughter was sweet,
as you upstaged my entrance,
all eyes were on you,
you were dressed to the nines
in surveillance camera blue.
The downside of perfume, displayed here

in guillotine chic
wraps weight round your jewel box
it is thrown from a bridge
measured serpentine waistlines
emotional invalids.

Party RSVPs burned on tenement steps
and the ashes all mix with the guests and the fixtures
great ghosts of less virtue
were no less persistent.

In the guests' rooms unreality,
visitors and vanity
playing games with light
it's you against the mirror
and your audience
and all you do is fraudulent.

About the Beauty of Laura

About the beauty of all above everything,
all about the fire escapes and elevators
conceding to waste our time on the ground,
for a passage to claim back our altitude,
whereupon the air might be thin,
but who said that breathing
was one of the things
we were interested in.
About the caves
where our puzzled expressions reflect
generating light on the walls,
pictures flicker and fall,
just changing the story enough
to give resolve to us all.

Oh, about the beauty of Laura,
something waits to begin
where the beauty steps in
and the girls have a wonderful day
capsizing the men.
All that flickers and falls looks like Laura,
don't you know the role she reprised
has that look in her eyes
her expression won't change
as she wilfully writes out the men.

All about the beauty
of silent eyed symphonies,
too scared to breathe loud for discord
mismanage the words
and all time will distort
you lunge forward to claim your reward,
trust is broken
and precious stones fall to the ground,
gain strength as patterns they form,
and your aim is disarmed,
the crime of all secrets is lost
in your composite charm.
Seek the beauty in pictures of Laura relaxed,
in a hand movement she flies
with her arms open wide
her failure to touch the ground
heightens what we must decide.

Fortune Strikes Again

It's your favourite role to be in,
it's your favourite game to play,
dare I ask you to participate in hindsight?
For a figure to display,

long enough to learn of leaving,
with a forced apology,
slow enough to stare you down by way of blindness,
you refuse delivery.

Consider what we'll be without,
slide across the ice
without the belief to support you,
a late comer you can't see without,
oh, fools rush to get rid of fleeting moments to adore you.

Fortune strikes again,
but you must encourage him to hold you,
not a witness, not a friend,
but the first to second guess the end.

But I have no pride to speak of,
but to drain off some of yours,
steal the moment and replace it with a lifetime,
this kind of thief is insecure,
had enough, so here's your answer,
cry it tough and wave bye-bye,
sick of traveling with uncertain looking strangers,
sick of leaving for a lie.

When lovers sink the last remaining ship,
oh, cargos, clustered millionaires
claim privilege to board you,
as the crow flies to our false intended target
feel the mouth that wants to kiss you
sinking sand upon the shore.

Fortune strikes again,
but you must encourage him to hold you,
not a witness, not a friend,

but the first to second guess the end.

My fortune imprecise, I'm giving up on love
no steps to paradise, I'm giving up on love
no habit, no surprise, I'm giving up on love
no risk or certainty, I'm giving up on love.

Lipstick in Labyrinth Park

A good night for lipstick,
covert meetings in the park,
is that an angel hiding in the branches of birches?
Her halo's alight,
but her face is obscure by the dark,
I'll meet you in mazes my love,
it's just the safest place to be,
don't be alarmed if you think you can't find me,
I'm round every corner,
be patient and wait there for me,
a good night for perfume predictions,
my fictitious accomplice is wearing a dress,
coloured sweet by the moon,
off her slim frame it falls,
then the light kissed her skin,
I submerge in her anthems and labyrinths,

Motion feels cool on my face as I stumble to trace,
the words and the footsteps
back where the maze began,
try to replace that magic,
oh, what I never give away,
in time make it up to you,
I'm trying to get back,
I'm trying to get back,

Lipstick, labyrinths, leave me here,
I feel so close my dear,
in labyrinths,
trying to lose my way,
stars bright,
but it looks like the end of light,
so I'll follow your lead tonight,
baby, I'm trying to lose my way.

A good night for wearing it thin,
don't let anything settle
for less than you bargained,
peering eyes from persuasion
that's the price that you pay,
at least I was honest,
just didn't have the right words to say,
your face looks amazing, my love,
lips that shock me to sainthood,
with the force of a gun,
eyes where stars die of envy
to be reborn contently
in the palms of your hands
little jewels for your pleasure to throw.
A good night for breaking routine
as we rush round in circles
pretending we're thirteen,
the maze walls are see through
but they are misty from us
our initials on glass walls
connect until there's no maze at all.

No One is Scared

You threw a line,
you were blissful

as you fell into that oil, turpentine
just like wine
and your skin came to fruition,
and the rules all change again,
some submission
some reward,

So easy to hide when nobody's looking,
so easy to change when no one is scared,
nobody's scared,
nobody's frightened even when you change for good,
nobody's scared,
nobody's frightened even when you change for good.

Watching you win
all those races
that you cheated and lied to get in,
every day comes,
you must take some
and the rules all change again,
some are shattered,
some are whole,

Just think of the people you're trying to win over,
just think of the friends you're trying to win back...
nobody's scared,
nobody's frightened
even when you change for good,
nobody's scared,
nobody's frightened
even when you change for good.

The Last Hit Man in Heaven

You're the last one to go and walk into a room
picking out those saints
like they were walking home to soon,
cold blooded history on a rosary, yeah,
and heavenly triggers animosity.
To what do I owe these guilty pleasures to?
Do these sins precede a lesser elevation, I don't know,
save a place for me between god's invited answers
in rooms of atrophy all bled for leisure's sake,
he greets the hit man with the weapon of his choice,
acid, alkali or lipstick, but he doesn't have a voice.

And it never feels right, no
delivered safely, never shadow sanctified
what's there to say?
You might just…

Few decisions between heaven or a hitman,
I was kind of hoping there'd be room left just for one
but I don't see the skill of angels
stretch enough to silence every gun,
when you illuminate the passage to persuasion,
ghosts are reflected and they unlock every door
shadows weep, the hitman hides
behind the one you never locked before.

Hit by shadows last hitman
in heaven I don't think you can.

You're the one they voted "vandal lost in heaven"
replacing lullabies
with all the warpath reasons you were given
the beast that breeds caution and trains it to bite

any mile-long great mistakes
that will approach you here tonight.

Give it up—bite back
give it up—bite back
gotta give it up
but I'm so afraid to lie and bite back.

NIGHT OF YOUR LIFE

Too Long in My Mind

Through this fading glass I worship you
I've been too long in my mind
all the paintings and the obstacles
off them tears can only slide
when you look upon my grace parade
the year will never fade
dressed in female answers
swallow wingless blue
it changes while you wait
of all the strangest songs you're dancing to
you had to pick out this
its melody a corridor of speechless
its rhythm stringed with bliss
caught up briefly by a clumsy prince
lost arms and riddle signs
a miracle upon a silk charade
I've been too long in my mind.

You will sing, you will wingless sing
you will sing through no words
choose the one, choose the only one
who will fly with no birds.

Want to tell, but there is no tell
want to share, but there is no share
could I die without knowing you
I will die without showing you.

Don't Landslide Away from Me

Don't don't
don't you try to please
landslide away from me
landslide away from me
it's much too late to hide!
Be difficult, myth eyes
landslide away from me
landslide away from me.

Don't don't
looks that thread a river
thrown away from me
they're thrown away from me
the sea of caution dried
her pupils never wrote me why
away from me
landslide away from me.

Climbed the highest wall
made the buildings all
landslide away from me
and the television rolled
it broadcast all my biggest faults away from me
landslide away from me.

Don't don't
believe the starlet's injured
she's your sister now
she's got a pretty mouth
her taxi waits outside
she struck the city's underside
away from me,
landslide away from me.

But don't don't
operation "dig for secrets"
hear from me, you will not hear from me
brunette October beach
her smirky birth is out of reach
away from me
landslide away from me.

Climbed the highest wall
made the buildings all
landslide away from me
and the television rolled
it broadcast all my biggest faults away from me
landslide away from me.

Lowbrow swordfights
in the stairwells rust,
a man on fire will magnify you,
light devices in the evening hush
and if you're tired, we'll try to wake you.

Volunteers for valentines will burn you up
the rock of age will grate your nerves a lot
sliding sad requests make innocents corrupt
landslide mind's a joke we heard a lot.

Night of Your Life

The flaws in your late night
they will shake in the height of your tenement sky
bracing the wasted as
they slice through the roofs
they just want to drop by
a card was delivered
but the name was withheld

too much news for a newborn
surround and endeavour
and they fall like the weather
all but fire to a form.

A newly built statue
with contrition for eyes
blurs the story I told
burned and unrested
hammer hands are drug tested
no more money will fold
so corpse-lit the path
drives you right off the map
it's the night of your life
so breathe your own shadow
and drink to the wasted
it's the night of your life.

Wasted the wall stops weeping
in all the excitement
the night of your life burns a hole
questions and time,
never figure declined
as you wake back to dawn.

Low amongst nightlife
so you figure skate home
no more injured than blessed
these wheels are a curse
they divide you the worst
but they lap-dance the best
extremes of compassion
are wrapped around dagger eyed
issues of force,
unmasked and unfortunate,

miles to the exit
disabled of course.

Those streams of collapse
still extreme in their fast-tracks
go unmeasured and blind
a throwback to the worthless
or the fashions of gold
bullets sewn to the mind
desired point of impact
levels last standing bridges
mirrored river release
pulled back skin barrier
instead of a dam
now I'll never find peace.

Stella (Stand Up and Take Your Man)

Stella,
words too slow will not stand straight,
working back to a reason
that all ends can breathe on,
don't hesitate,
you stand up to disguise
all that was paradise in your stolen purse,
and the lights when you misread
the words here instead
only make things worse.

Bella and her balancing act
and we all fall down,
Stella and her look of surprise
when the dancers hit the ground.

Stella—stoic motion,

adrift when you work that hard,
I just got a message
that's still convalescing between two stars,
if the mood's still elated,
it's just badly translated,
it can't rise to fight,
yes, the feeling's low
and the drinks still flow,
we're still up with night.

Bella and her balancing act
and we all fall down,
Stella and her look of surprise
when the dancers hit the ground.
Stand up and take your man,
don't be afraid all the time,
'cos I'm the only one you're seen with, it's sublime,
and that's a bad, bad sign.

Stella stands so close to me
it's a breaking game!
Her nerves are all black
just like silver spoiled
by a naked flame,
if her world is a peepshow,
the camera's slow
like a creeping mist,
and the film's all projected like turmoil,
unsounded and fathomless.

Glass Rose

The game is etched in sand for you,
like a joke from above the punchline,
sandstorms and ill-lit faces grew

foreign dancers,
focused artifice,
makes the art of it too cruel.

Should I make my hands respond?
Like a mine of uncut jewelry,
no bones,
no ice to break the storm,
but I promise you,
yeah, I promise where I'm from,

Everything that you waited for,
is right here baby
right behind this open door,
come to this
like you did before.

Nicola Six

Oh, this is Nicola
follows her own footsteps
lifetime of agendas
much too fast
to wait for high heels to collapse,
god, she's wicked,
crippled foxtrot wicked
London intuition
foreign accent
from a sexy British kill,
Ooh la la!
she's shiny, in a drunken pilot rage
solitaire with screwdrivers
you'll wait there for an age,
face upturned,
to the puppet mistress silhouette,

love is burned,
like the end of Nicky's cigarette,

Walk up the stairs
the tenant, she invites you,
but she's not where she's supposed to be
and I just stare
in my uninvited way,
in my uninvited way,
Nicola Six, she'll burn you with a cigarette.

Nicola Six, imaginary friend
destroy the men and drink them under
any table low enough,
their heads are bowed
do you notice
how brutal strength just shies away
her beauty, her resources
burning up the ones she sends away,

Oh my my!
The innocence and black of lingerie
her skirt is touched
by a man who wants to be her for a day
face upturned
to the hand that wants to slap you
skin is burned (unconcerned)
by the cigarette she dropped...

Roullettescape

Let's join forces, I'm an emergency
in the roullettescape, blind visits beneath what's fate
first the endangered when they are strangers here
spinning roullettescape, all the force minus majesty.

Never call on people forced to face what rings
in the roullettescape, oh
not like finders/keepers ache too steep designs
in the roullettescape, oh

Terrace sprayed with gold (it's getting better, oh it's getting better)
all skinless hands to hold (is it me, oh better, I believe it's getting
    better)
fight of a lifetime falls (it's hitting harder, I believe it's getting
    better)
get out the roullettescape doubt (rolling harder, oh it's getting
    better)
drop like the odds all faceless frauds...

In walks time with electric urgency
god and roullettescape, gates scraping for a fading lock
mocking pickpockets freeze through the flightless air
in the roullettescape, glass ashes on a butcher's block

Knee high dancers in a faceless anti-spin
spinning roullettescape, oh
ghost casino sightings flee with dancers' speed
in the roullettescape, oh

Lace with light dissolved (it's getting better, oh it's getting better)
piano wires to hold (is it me oh better, I believe it's getting better)
paper blood from the dealer's hands (pouring harder, I believe it's
    getting better)
no sense of roullettescape doubt
(getting louder, oh it's getting better)
drop like the odds all faceless frauds...

Respond to Beauty

I don't wanna play a game
project on the wall and I could have looked better
but the lines remain the same
black and white over rocks and steam, lord
makes me feel like some trick photographer's idea
of a never open door

And the words they just will you to live
like some high above you consul
love's a mockery of everything

I don't wanna play a game,
respond to beauty
like its name was never changed
I don't wanna play a game

Even crisis left alone
falling cradle of injured
like a frost to the ghost
of "I'll never be alone"
Is there time to make you mine?
In the film I pretend,
but I will love you 'til the end
of a film that's never mine

Carriage wheels turn and beg you to stay
curse the want of new arrivals
I wish I'd never talked to anyone

I don't wanna play a game
respond to beauty
like its name was never changed
I don't wanna play a game

On the cinema screen,
I run like I wrote the scene
to a place where the actors brave,
an off-camera grave
your five-mile wall—or maybe just the stories tall…
I'll second guess and reach the top,
to watch the audience drop
the crime stands still,
the detective, he just lost his will
responds to beauty like a 911,
he's got his hand on his gun

I cannot call to you
your feeding, laughing, breaking voice in two,
just respond it through
and when it changes, oh, the midnight saint estranged
and hours left, so go back, go back, please make it true.
Cold as it might be,
a distance spared converts the strangely beautiful
back through that glass with you,
cold as it might be,
when death ignites me
destined to elaborate
back through that glass with you…

Cartwheel Proposal

A sword-swallowing fool
repairs a balloon
all that he may
destroy it again.
A creature
described on the posters in town
"not since the bible… etc"
come around.

The lions and priests
they circle the dead
one teaches the other
about prayer before bloodshed
a fresh disgraced pilot
gives lessons in weightless
how to fall and be silent
whilst playing with your fate

Afraid that her jewelry
gets lost in the grass
care falls in abandon
she is rolling too fast!
Brown paper and vinegar
to ward away danger
and granite surprises
of skull-fractured splendour

Proposal of hijinx
to the fire breathing failures
the flawed entertainers
the kings for a day,
the "always the bridesmaids"
with bouquets of nuisance
the down at mouth jugglers
who beg you to stay

I drew it up—a cartwheel proposal
a game we can play
in the fields for a day
no hopscotch monstrosity
call Catriona and Allison
Roseanne, take a bubble bath
we didn't invite you

we didn't invite you
we didn't invite you
go away

Stevie Smith

It's too far, it's not easy
horse widths to the shore
unsteady bridge
coast layers
acrobats worth saving
sandstorms to remind us
Stevie Smith

THE EPISODES

Mirror Lips

It's unlikely that you will remember
the text that reflected on you
I'm coming to grips with your mirror lips
I can read all about me on you
it's quite an incredible story
you hold it so close to your face
a solar eclipse of indifference it shines
on the dusty remains of this place

Looking glass vacuum conditions
the questions I'm dying to ask
the lips can't accuse, they'll cut open themselves
the face can't agree it's a mask
You're standing behind every doorway
absorbing the neighbours' distress
the writings reversed and the story's perverse
the finale's a stain on your dress

Grace is frozen like wax in a whirlpool
your danger face warns us too slow
talk crawls like a mist
and ignores an agreement
just digs for an insult to throw
cremated like all of your diaries
the language remains obsolete
it was once on cassettes but they've since dried and perished
became the sand under your feet

It's unlikely, it's all in your mind
it'll blow the day out of the water

unlocking the doors,
drop on wet Roman floors,
mirror lips, but the text is distorted and listless
we'll polish it offthat's it, we'll polish it off

Your mirror lips blowing out smoke rings
from cigarettes, disasters or guns
they hang in the air like the Baptists hair
dispersed in the light of the sun
your mystery penetrates cities
pre-emptively ridicules myths
risk everyone's necks by reversing the text
spitting back with your mirror lips

The Son of Empty Sam

We'll force it back in fathoms
what we forced back to decay
your life and times in questions
rain forced too black to stay
you mirrored out your reasons
before you disappeared
when sequence eyes destroyed you
you grew back out of fear

D'you think I know conditions
of ice and metal grey
the lipless lakes before you
will suffocate their prey
I cut down all my friends
to see where I might lie
on simple blades of unlit truth
the truth will bleed you dry

A dog bites the owner

to remind him of his pain
father's dragged by horses
to remind him why he came
a lion's share of breakneck
SUPERSTITIOUSLY
exposed flame to a life force
it's creeping back to me.

Can still be thoughts of murder
down there with empty Sam
colliding with your mistrust
the operation lands
between two styles of envy
one old, one late for church
the messages they send me
glow far more than they're worth

Don't dream no eyeless dream
'cos you might wake up blind
your hands around a stranger's throat
reborn the killing kind
rotating quotes are worthless
confuse the best of me
my fists are empty curses
they can't just wait and see

From wicked blue there hangs a rock
to make your god stand straight
you find you can't rebuild your world
collapsing from its weight
an antique box of questions
conceivably for you
looks down on my reflection
it does not mean it's true

Feels like you're out there moving
in the frozen air for me
dead sculptures to ice cultures
no more second sight disease
it's darkest in the morning
light dropping down in poles
shards metal evening
when dawn gets too close

Like coal in some forgotten mine
black diamond memories
all blood runs black with the lights out
it still feels warm to me
the coast of attrition
Atlantic blueprint crime
submerge in forest anger
you'll always wake up blind

For the sake of the no answers
penetrate the air in flames
falls scorching from an unnamed cloud
an unread list of names
of who can move like midnight
the son of empty Sam
and who can prove the others wrong
before the flames began

I CAN'T GO HOME

Every Ghost Has an Orchestra

Every ghost has an orchestra,
just to spoil your aim at sunset,
famished white,
stained by coruscating light

all those flickering sand dunes
diamond holes upon the paper
see you later
don't have any time for you

To move or take sides in a war?
And you're starving
can't go very far
midnight drowned in this song
I would teach, but you'd sing it wrong
you're falling lashes and I-beams
wet skin from that mystery steam
slip and slide
every door pushed open wide

Every ghost and its cache of helpers
you can't see them but you fall in love
rust on surface
you contain no purpose
see the sign outside of the mission
eyes are wide, but you never listen
orchestrated
you just stood and waited

In a manner of speaking I grew up
left all waking life behind me
so inside me,
I could never think again,
Every ghost holding fast to a theme song
I let go: I have never been strong
something conjured
from the needful and the injured
stories stole from beyond the witness
the indignant mistaken for gifted
gracious force

that obscures the screen of course
every overture deployed from your lips
scattered stones upon the high road
look the same
when we hear those strings again
you run startled to hide from the high notes
you roar from your low-end throat
"where went the safety,
that I could walk on every road?"
You tried to tell me there exists a wish list
and every flight of every ghost
oh, you'll never catch a shadow
you will never get to move that close
never thriving for the sake of the certain
smoke black shiver and shake of emblems
the young disguise mistakes in a minefield
the orchestra pastoral and slow,
mimics every sweep of every searchlight
every orchestrated knock on the door
every fake "congratulations"
invitations that you choose to ignore.
And you can't discard your crimes in the water
the harbour lights will take care of that
screaming guilty, your filthy
with a history of crime............
And in my house there are obstacles
just like relay races to dead ends
get down on all fours
bathe in the light from under doors
never live for your indecision
the first chair on your dying lips
all the strings bend
look while the woodwind sinks your ships
trace all that light from a double helix
all the pattern of the shade in a key change

rolling minors, distant signs
overture designers
EVERY GHOST HAS AN ORCHESTRA
while raining doubt upon your soundtrack
just the last gasp
the last movement, don't look back

Henry Versus Miller

I'm too precise, looking backwards,
no one's that nice,
fireless clothed luxury, you'll never be mine,
frayed like the rope that suspended your curtains,
soaked like a sail on your sinking ship
best before metaphors
carry your weight
like a cross up that hill.

Jealous the love in a laughing triangle
three ways to escape
stuck in the middle, or dead in the wings
where fatigue made you wait,
a day without air as you're leaving the country,
a day without light as it pulls you downhill
spangle-eyed tropics content to stare
but you never know where

as the last sin belt-clips to your wasteland
as the last pistol's happy new year
it's a cold one
you're just an old one
a show of hands for everyone you see
congratulations, they are all like me
now slowly as the verses you translate
now slowly as the verses

slowly as the verses
slowly as the verses
slowly as the verses

Before they intrude
you can screen your own childhood on the back of a coin
when focused light dazzles, you remember it all
the hysterics and joy
a three-angled park burns the myth of all sunlight
you got bit by a dog, 'cos you kept your eyes closed
wall to wall dark, or the prize of a fighter
crawl past the mark, a disqualified race

Lost track of all time, we cascade through the New Town,
each infatuates the other one home
where at this time, can we shoplift survival?
Where at this time can we leave us alone?
Clatter of heels on the stairs in the garden
shine like the wheels on the taxi we lost,
the last dance was slick, like the oil on your Pernod,
frightened, it moved
like a phantom on frost...

Soul Boys/Hard Legends

Soul boys/hard legends
revolve around the city tonight
to penetrate separate
deluxe and the desperate
the legend never they were right
close shave/Valentino's
we sounded an alarm on the street
the mystery medallion men
and disco girls anonymous
the Friday night forever elite

Live wire/soul dancing
the 70s behind us again
it's always so impossible
to stare down your partner
it's Leith Walk in the 80s my friend

I wish/my darling
but nostalgia's just a bit like revenge
the smoke that spells distress
from your JPS
burns like our Friday night
'til the end
soul boys/hard legends
square go's the length of Lothian Road
abandoned bags or araldite
diffuse the rained-on perfume
they're shouting
and they're dancing in code

Concerns
modern nite life
a neon timebomb
stretched like the truth
rotating sleepwalk accurates
doing speed in the bathroom
1980 81 82

Work like a hero
you're peeling back the streets you adore
you don't need a map
to deliver the distance
you don't need any light anymore
the frames of buildings
are trafficking electrical ghosts
surrounded in fiction

of soul boy's survival
to buy into the legend the most

Notes for a screenplay
we're bringing back the city to life
on top of the playhouse
in Princes Street Gardens
30 frames a second tonight

Empty Coda

It was in the cards
assumed before you, anyway
remembering the son of empty Sam
we're forcing the fathoms
we're further back, anyway
remembering the son of empty Sam
coal leaves the mine at the altar here, anyway
ring of the diamond memory
blood's running black in the midnight,
it's warm to me
remembering the son of empty Sam.

FORGIVENESS & EXILE

Arran

The walls of Ardrossan
make for colourless wheels,
slowed down as the gulls spill sound
and the ferryboats reel.
Minute is the mainland
and the Holy Isle shines,
through a cave made of clouded eyes
and warning signs.

Made skill of the night life
but I can see how it could have made you hide,
make it home again, or never leave me,
and the worth remains inside,
the patterns on Lamlash are the scars on Whiting Bay,
I know I'm going to die on Arran
I just don't know on what day.

When you're down on the low tide
you can walk to where you want,
standing stones-west coast at midnight,
where the basking sharks have sunk
when the mad shine of a lighthouse
interrupts the midnight view
makes the drunk fall off the Brodick pier
and the drunk is always you.

The map that you read can't betray the height
of how the gardens became foothills
and the foothills might be as close to any heaven
anyplace you wish to pray,

there's no Arran without endless love
no other place I wish to stay.

Forgiveness & Exile

Forgiveness and exile,
partially to blame
a need to go to this place
to do it all again
in sorrow, few surprises
dripping wet endeavoured paths
even soldiers become exiles
dying letters home at last.

The space between dead air
all flash united by a beam
its flicking caught the edge of a corpse
and the violence in between
the lights will probe a fractured war
by feeling in the dark
relief maps or just open sores
dismemberment as art.

The closeness of the needles,
consuming empty rooms,
black bulbs cast ink and shadows
forgiveness afternoon,
the vapour in the trenches,
is mercy met with awe,
prying eyes through loopholes watch,
the silence of the war,
misshapen lead contraptions,
try to lope across the fields,
through severed crops of human end,
the blood becomes congealed,

the exile from a bottle dropped,
evaporates to air,
decelerates the whiskey drench,
infirmary and fear.

Forgiveness and exile,
hid in the corner shakes,
and shock becomes transmission,
a thunder through the lakes,
sends famished birds in shrieking arcs,
away from feast and field,
risk takers to the sun advance,
while all the fighters kneel.

The cold blood of morning
makes a red mask of dawn,
turns black birds into red avengers,
and the wind they fly upon,
the fields are never green,
just made of starving scars of soil,
where broken feathers clash with snares,
in swamps of frozen oil.
Jet arcs of fuel salute the clouds,
gushed from the cracked machines,
in flames, in celebration,
in black smoke cloud extreme,
you may have seen some stagger,
broken lope between the hoofs,
upturned like bony smokestacks,
built on top of winter roofs,
you may have seen some stealthy!
As they fearful scan the length,
too prone, even with a smoke disguise,
too long without their strength,
you may have seen some aiming,

to the birds, with homemade guns,
some cancered flesh to gnaw on,
some bullets to outrun.

Cross another makeshift bridge
perception has no depth
it is spun out across two canyons
from unfinished buildings
and unfinished steps
wood hammered together
like lies in a disqualifies dialogue
shiver splinters walk the plank
projecting easy gaits
exile daubed by fresh strawberries
adorn the prison hands
WORLD WAR II
THE CRIMEA
CULLODEN
BOER
...ROSES!

Clouds without pity

The resurrection at sea
as spirits parade
submerged on sandbanks,
you listen to the shell's heart worn ballads and eulogies,
half roared at low volume,
the people have been too frightened to swim,
the dead sea had us all humbled at high tide,
leveled at low tide,
rumours of islands
and disappearing craft,
legends of clouds without pity,
and force without mercy,

have brought me here—and now I idle,
the pushing and the shaking of fake equators
has made me become with the sea—all undertow, peaks and
    troughs,
bully the languid limbs whilst the persistent channels
trespass into yawing vein and usher out panicked blood,
the pores on blue white skin,
eroded to herald in the tempest.
Of all seas, the dead sea
but at least I am here,
at least it can't hurt me,
now it has consumed me.

The surgery

Bent black by inefficiency
and bent back by innocence
the muscles across the sky
cast turn of the 20th
moving picture shadows
over the scope of the moors
half-finished buildings on the scape of the moors
their feebly united woods and wires
stretching like a zealot's arms to heaven
diseased foundations
creeping
with the atrophied roots of trees
apprehensively downwards
futile search for a drink in the loam
moore is a smug adversary
mouth alive with set traps and frights
the nesting pheasant
the WWII subterranean bomb shelter
now blown open
and waiting to devour our

frightened night-time exiles
smoke on the moor by some drastic fire
the black matching the sky punch for punch
the quarry almost illuminated
by partial flashes
slide they down shale
to the lake at the bottom
clay clouds
that no living thing
may imbibe of its air
FORGIVENESS AND EXILE
apologies buoyed by their own savage velocity
ricochet feverishly
across sky made of war
the open mouths of castles
hacking coughs
APOLOGY NOT ACCEPTED
that words become soldiers
that soldiers become words
a sentence contradicted
before it was formed
legions of affliction
secrets battle axed
and dragged into
the surgery of waking hours
punctuation expels meaning
and we are
left with pauses and anchors.

The wallet

Walking carefully,
around a small island
more of a giant rock in the sea,
you are looking, but you never return

to the point where your craft
is supposed to be moored.
Grey slick rock decorated
with former grass adornment
wind and kelp
you think you know
because you used a rusty mooring ring
that protruded from a rock
you do not remember any tide,
nor wind,
nor sun,
or rain
there was no weather
it was afternoon
the sea not perilous
but a restless sleeper
it was afternoon.

The hill was difficult to scale,
not because of its steepness
but the nature of the way the thick, copse
grass grew,
obscuring the many rocks and rabbit holes,
meaning that you would trip all the time,
your ankles would twist,
or you would hurt your wrist.
The building at the top
must have been some sort
of lookout post, or bunker the walls are thick and although doorless
    and windowless,
there was a small entrance, and two slits cut
into the cement.
The afternoon air was still and claustrophobic
both outside and in,
as you walked in, you could see on the cement floor,

evidence of a small fire,
the walls covered with what looked like aerial photographs
of the wilderness where you had been walking.
It had clearly been recently vacated.

You are about thirty feet from the body
it lies on the other side of the house
in the pocket of the corpse's jacket
there is a wallet that you know contains money, however, traversing
the floor to reach the body will be excruciating, because most of
the floor has been either pulled up by prior looting, or burnt in
the inevitable fire.
The room is dark save for occasional sparks that spit from garrotted
wires, rusted non-specific devices and appliances.
This makes the work more acutely dangerous, as every surface is
slick from combustible agents and fuel,
to reach the coveted wallet, you have to crawl along the remaining
planks, trying not to touch the wires,
and trying not to slip off the planks into the abyss of the basement,
from which you can hear a faint scraping and shaking sound.
You crouch and bend forward.
The planks are long and thin.
And with such little support, there is nothing
to stop them from bending drastically in the middle.
You inch forward slowly, without breathing.
Your pores filled with chemicals.
The random sparks angrily spit and scorch.

After about 15 minutes there is a snap
and the corpse falls from the ledge it was balanced upon
and into the basement.

No myths or stars

In the dream,
low tide is neither land nor water,
but the purgatory between,
without any resolution,
you are walking,
feeling your way down a meandering corridor
walled by wire rusted to a blackened auburn,
now that the moon no longer turns the tides: without light
the only sensation is when the salt enters the cuts on your feet,
deeper hypnotized by the freezing wave's persuasion—"come to us"
low tide prolongs the journey—of all seas—but it does not matter,
    this could be any of them or none
no sirens or triangles,
no tridents or sharks,
or stars no myths to guide to as your limbs, exhausted from fear,
    turn to sleep for an answer.

Or stars no myths to guide to as your limbs, exhausted from fear,
    turn to sleep for an answer.

No myths or stars to guide to as your limbs, exhausted from fear,
    turn to sleep for an answer
now you are all sea.

The water has failed us:
seething dialects under a reclusive sky,
aerial view of a submerged staircase,
iron rings,
chains and crippled anchors,
the water failed—its buoyancy replaced by cold, indifferent stoicism
that cares not about the inevitable bridge suicide,
or the toxic tributaries,
its opaque duty to curate its dead collection,

of gulls, skulls and brined devices,
a spectator might see refracted riches,
submerged in exile
closely knit with pauses of stretching sand.

Of all seas

…And why *should* I wake up anywhere less treacherous?
…and why *shouldn't* I be adrift in walls of fog, and a ceiling of hail?

The floor, an event of the occasion of wreck splinters and snapped
    masts,
the chorus, an avian mob hushed not by these waves,
scissor winds cut the strings of north and south, east and west,
fray and snap, until there is no direction.
And where were we, if not marching en masse?
If memory serves (which it doesn't)
I am barely aware of my neighbour's presence, alive or dead, in the
    water with me, neither close nor far.

I shouldn't float for long, I know it is the dead sea,
but I carry the weight of a traitor, and, as you know
treachery begets treachery.

Of all seas, anonymous gales that could grant safe passage
instead break your heart in the every direction—the wings,
the sails,
crests of waves like soldiers,
troops of sanguine ambush,
out there to lap below the anchor ropes,
the miracle of withered mystery,
the succour of summer's secret
"how late it is, how late it is, how late it is"
trying to commit my initials to the water,
so dense with salt,

avoiding the light,
the story is passed around or down,
changing every time with the subtleties of coral and whirlpools,
and I became one such whirlpool,
one such vortex,
I was water in reverse,
my fingers all over the dead sea,
clawing and clutching the hardness of the fights as they ended
in astonishment, in anguish,
my legs around myths,
stopping the flow of their blood,
the last is spoken with frustration and defeat—of all seas, the dead
    sea.

The slow motion birds

Forgiveness and exile
permanent stain on your lenses
peripheral obscured
by slow motion birds
the mystery excels
obscures what you have imagined
dismisses that to which you aspire
risk takers towards the sun advance
alchemists whose formulas are ashes
mediums whose skills exclude the dead
snipers under the reign of the misfire.

Days between visions

In these days between vision,
your hand that dissected the ocean,
that force fed an era of answers,
so broken,
slow motion,

those lines between islands,
the orbiting ash,
present gifts on your beaches,
of dubious worth,
this here is a gull,
five days dead by submerging,
this might have been glass from a bottle,
now rounded-smooth enough to swallow,
a rope wrapped with seaweed,
like the opposite of flags,
alongside comes THE DOGS
hands digging for sandworms,
while they churn up a jawbone,
half-grinning, half mimicking,
for the key to the island,
when the tide is up high,
is the inverse of a pattern
on the beach where it lies.

This is sand just like years,
between the wrecks of machine works,
quietly praised and high held,
like volcano-torn church bells,
while the sea howls its psalms,
it will bite back the beaches,
reclaiming its gifts,
like a petulant child,
there are walls around this ocean,
for privacy's sake,
and they look like the islands,
gnawed through by us gannets!
Sword swallowers in granite!
There is none that will trespass,
as we soak our fiestas,
great minds will meander,

like bullies on treadmills,
and we move just like sharks,
too exultant for danger,
nothing gets in the way
when the heart is displayed,
forgiveness is hidden
while the exile prays.

This is sand just like hours,
pouring as redemption,
onto the beached corpses,
as far as the horizon,
like a bloated and decaying Braille
message to our minder.

Obsolete weapons
long rusted by brines,
stubborn the trigger
in a time wasted war,
random the graveyard
unplanned execution,
mottled meat feathers,
endangered species,
erupt and eclipsed,
forward, estranged weatherless day,
hungry and stubborn
birdies of prey,
climb frightened down cliff,
stamp careless on every bird's nest,
mottled red sand,
mottled red script,
the curving of the limbs,
underscores all,
with a flourish,
the deadbeats in the craters

under birdies of prey,
stranded strands of sinew,
become one with the worms,
in an effort to choke
all of the birds.

This is sand just like seconds,
blown to dry out the foliage,
bullet strength splinters,
speed of light scars,
the mysteries
kept in a solid smoke vertigo,
older than ashes,
younger than wars,
the preaching of the air,
just howls confession,
from the fixtures and dunes,
stand still, bright machinery,
stand still, Angelus bells,
great minds still meander,
their discoveries
a secret
in low-tide forests of kelp
busied
by mid afternoon
weatherless ebb,
FORGIVENESS AND EXILE
even here, on the beach,
the sweetness
hidden in a smooth blue glass heart,
sent painfully above an ocean,
like the moments between Shetland storms,
even here,
war is a tight-lipped séance,
"forgiveness and exile"

even here.

This is sand just like centuries,
when all is forgiven,
still raining from the hourglass,
the dunes still as prison walls,
the arenas are for fighting,
round, like a lens in the sun,
as the competition marches
point blank to your zero,
the circling hunger
just howls like an audience,
try to determine each weight of each cry,
each muscle of the language,
too tired to communicate,
no longer exiled,
but your will-it remains so,
prone, like an "x" in the sand,
defying any water, to fall on this land,
the dulled overview,
presents only spectres of a life,
RED-ADRIATIC-CASPIAN-DEAD.
Move like the ghost of the dead air,
measured steps,
and fatal betrayal.

This is sand from the centre,
curved fracture of the world,
the steam that lies beneath the sea,
the broken window passage,
glass reflection of the landscape,
these are more than injured times,
the tidal inches towards total,
the tide inclined where it can't find.
Time slipped in the fractured world,

hidden by curls of steam,

they trace out a map of affliction,

and it matches the city's disguise,

now owned by the frightened in the margins,

bathing their fear,

in the space between storms,

the chorale that you breathe to,

the chorale that you breathe against,

walks out of the air,

and undresses in front of you,

triumph and funeral,

ghost of the air,

wretched crippled clothes,

decorate iron dark water,

Ophelia's opposite,

with a blue-black grin,

the stars, and the last of the electric light,

pick out and reverse the features,

gluttony of theatre,

blue black and grinning again,

hand claw attack pose,

like the monger just froze,

flat against frame,

the background to paintings,

skill of the pardons,

you will not hear again,

the sutures unreason,

but they punctuate skin,

illustrating the fracture of world,

no more severe skies,

no more air,

as the insects multiply and ignite,

no more air,

no more air,

no more air.

I know what I've seen, and I know what is coming, and some of it will be quite beautiful...

Only an omen, but THAT omen,
criss-cross coal bars against your sky
mining the sky,
ladders and pulleys
volleying sunset to ground.
the light broad as it brushstrokes the victims
and champions the dark.

The buildings are destroyed, but at least they are buildings
laced and surrounded
by the predatory ghosts, of dead dictators-
burning and the looting of air
armed robbery of the airless,
lungs collapsed in unison and filled with oil,
roads of the city and beyond
pulled up like a dragnet
and swept over our surroundings
plucking them dry...
the bones grey-green stationary shadows
while the sun is in repose.

You are one who walks here,
a history without timeline,
a future without prediction,
and you say:

"I KNOW WHAT I'VE SEEN,
  AND I KNOW WHAT IS COMING,
  AND SOME OF IT WILL BE QUITE BEAUTIFUL"

PENTLAND FIRTH HOWL

The Fidra Birds

I barely mind that night
we drove into the sea in a low tide light
you said, "this is no place for our ride"
I said, "who cares where it is after a suicide?"
you scrambled for the 10 silk cut
the bottle of bells, and the rifle butt
I said, "Morag, slow down, I'm only joking around"
but you couldn't wait to use that gun
said you were tired of the silence
and the setting sun
there's barely breath where there was words
like they've been washed away and eaten by the Fidra birds
we laughed and stumbled out the car
the dawn was penetrating through a ghostly haar
I slashed into a rockpool, you slugged from the bottle
then we walked into the waves holding hands…

I think we'd been awake for days
and we'd barely said a word except for when we'd prayed
the streets so hushed, deferential to us
or as dead as the love we slayed
a decision was reached at one
we should both go out driving with my hunting gun
we could maybe go to Gullane
or North Berwick Law
but I want to see this out by dawn
and then an explosion of gulls
their shrieking as plaintive children of war
then Fidra just fell out the forth
our eyes so alight we just lit up the north.

With all the gallows humour spent
could we do it and make it look like an accident
she said, "You're the last boat in the harbour, son, I thought ye'd
    made it clear"
you can try to find the north star but just now it isn't near, and
    these decisions will be made by other people, just not us.

I was scunnered to see her gone
like the end of an eclipse of light that never shone
she was face down from me
rifle useless in the sea,
water played in caves in her skull
the echo of the act exiled the frightened gulls
and it exiled her man
I knew I couldn't drive
the car was sunk in sand
will I swim out to Fidra and hide?
the rocks they won't conceal me but the feathers might
but I never swam that well
and my lungs they filled with water
and a darkness fell
calling out to the Fidra birds…

The Felled Wych Elm
(Sighting of a Ghost at Bavelaw)

How harried we tramped through the black afternoon
the stones clawed our feet
all summer's great ramblings now frozen by rain
fast turning to sleet
you held up a finger, you pointed and yelled
at the elm it did fall
the ravens and craws
frightened out of their homes
and away from it all

I thought it got colder
and a figure did walk
from the elm and away
a ghost or a hermit on land made for no one
you whispered to me
we listened to nothing
the birds werenae talking
the rain had all stopped
too dark to feel safe
and too light to hide quickly
we just stood our ground
all the trees that span Bavelaw
could have fallen at that time
and you wouldn't hear a sound

As we try to find light
as we weave through the trees
the oaks and the wych elms, Alison and me
Bavelaw is haunted
and lost there are we
trying to get home for our tae

The day was so rare
as we walked over there
from the cottage at noon
the skies held the land
with their grey muscled hands
the wind breathed a tune
the strewn about neeps
and the fodder in heaps
the horses eclipse
there flanks to the gale
and their hoofs in the shale
while I kissed her lips
we climbed and we walked

way past three of the clock
then we stopped in the trees
I pissed on an oak
and you giggled and joked
then we both felt unease
all the leaves they did shake
as we lived our mistake
there was no going home
if Bavelaw is haunted
then we are both too
left out here alone.

Aberlour Aberlour

Aberlour love,
it's not like the first time,
the change invades my heart,
it swings like a bough,
dispersing canaries,
ambassadors of stars,
they'll find you where you are, do do do do

Aberlour love,
it's framed like a picture,
a hypnotizing sketch,
from quills and from oils
resolved in a vortex,
on pages etched in gold,
they'll find us I am told, do do do do

The rain obscured
by avalanches of celestesall playing scales of wonder
round and round
the strings implore the choir
to sing what can't be sung

and hold that note forever
round and round
round and round

I pray we're the same
I pray we are siblings
we breathe each other's past
it's built like a maze
that's flooded with fortune
the passages are pure
you'll find out when you're sure,
do do do do

Aberlour love,
comfort of the nameless,
I recognize your heart,
it mirrors my own
and all of the changes,
it quenches both our thirst
we'll find each other first.

An Accident in Scottish Wilderness

Take my side beneath the Scottish countryside
but you dream
the pity is not over
the wilderness becomes a dying soldier
weather knives, you ended up so desolate
the cairns and the corrosion
and the rest of it
but the glen is not a canyon it's a grave
just a subtlety of soul
between old waves

A measure of terror

ohh, your tongue-lashed hail
twists the road to liquid diamonds
man and animal impaled
old gods of bled out smoke horizons
angled now at flies
all the tales left on the mainland
all the closed doors and goodbyes

An accident in Scottish wilderness
there's nowhere to make history
there's no one else about
tell them I'm sorry
cover the site
we'll remain the same tonight

You never saw nothing
the landscape was still
but you felt the anger of the hills
the hole dug itself
and you climbed within it
how could you lie down there until…

Make your rain the mistake
as it batters the headland
make your fuck in the weatherland remorse
I could kill you for driving
but you thought of that first
an accident, a wilderness, a curse.

Goodbye, Waveland

Goodbye, waveland: no time, no history
no further north than I want to be,
goodbye, waveland: you won't respond to me
a finished heart with a starving past,

goodbye, waveland: drenched in sacrifice
drawing blood from a thing called love

I got up when I thought the boats had sailed,
to the shore with a gust of air,
I tried sinking surprise with a weight of sand,
disappointment to float my stare

Goodbye, waveland: you were my history,
and I'm too tired now to chase the tide,
goodbye, waveland: the birds are mourning me
you took the high road and I took the sea,
goodbye, waveland: you're god's celebrity
the shore's applause from the storm's encore

Got up to no good all the same old tricks,
took a drink and I almost drowned,
you don't know them like I do, the waveland days
on the estuary ground

Goodbye, waveland: you thought I'd follow you
but I can't live where I cannot see,
goodbye, waveland: the shear impermanence
jade shiny walls on a sculptured sea,
goodbye, waveland: I said goodbye my love
a threatened ocean on my second wind

Oh, I'm nearly seduced by the waveland look
and I turn and I smile away
and these etchings look grand on the night-time sand
in the morning, they're sad and grey...

Half in Light Arisaig Eyes

Half in light, you've been staring at sand,
turn it into a city by clutching your hand
the wrecks and the buildings, all disguised by lore,
the flight and the flightless, you shake and you soar.

Throwing gods off the islands
bringing rats to the rocks
all the iron ring jetties
and the dwindling flocks
every moment a morning
the Sabbath hid best
through the lines of the fences
submerged by the crests.

Half in light, half in light
half in light Arisaig eyes are what you stare through
when you write to disciples, you write to me too
the words and the circles from cliffs into caves
drown the signs and the prayers in the Arisaig waves
half in light, half in light.

Distant worths become seashells
collected in cups
by the kinder of castaways, gypsies and crofts,
they're displayed like a language,
sand like pages of gods
between desolate seaweeds and fulgurite rods.

Even gulls betray secrets
and cormorants lie
when the stones remain standing
the prayers will all die
you're betrayed by condition

no days between storms
no eyes between half light
to walk you back home.

Half in light, half in light
half in light Arisaig eyes are what you stare through
when you write to disciples, you write to me too
the words and the circles from cliffs into caves
drown the signs and the prayers in the Arisaig waves
half in light, half in light.

It Has Not Brought Me Peace

I walked round the island
and I traced out a map,
it was shaped like a cross
but I haven't found peace
and there were some women
and there were some sunsets
and there I did stand
but I haven't found peace

And time passed so quickly
in the black hole of America
I forgot who I was
and I never found peace
and lord, I have tried to acknowledge my birthplace
and remember my father
but I haven't found peace

And the climate did change in the 60s and 70s
and then I left my family
but I never found peace
and we were shattered
to each other we did scream

and I built my own fort
but I never found peace

And I walked and I walked
and the darker it got
the more I did stumble
and I never found peace
the claws of my conscience
they scratched at my memories
I'm a catholic and a coward
and I haven't found peace

There was solace in drugs
and in evil-eyed merchants
I was pleased to waste time
but I never found peace
and I walked through many lives
and locked the doors after me
and I never looked back
and I never found peace

When I swam back to the island
I was frozen mid-Atlantic
and I sank to the bottom
and I never found peace

And if I bring rain
that cascades on your heart
I sincerely apologise
but I haven't found peace
when I tried to find god
I was scared off by death
and I tried to forget
and I never found peace

Through clusters of trees
off high bridges I throw myself
and I'll always come back
but I haven't found peace
and I walk round the island
map bleached out by the sunshine
and I won't find my way
and I haven't found peace.

Ailsa Craig

You must be kind enough to escalate
the fever that you want so
to project up every rope
that fell from hidden scaffolding
on gallows and on carousels collect
A faintly cold anatomy that promises
the beaches that you hide on disappear
revealing nothing tangled
in survival slides
out of the sand it grew you
—the Pentland firth, it threw you

A name so silent that it's beautiful
it curls around you and it's all too brief
it drops like seasons born with clouded etiquette
a stare that doesn't question your belief

Contraptions built by us and pushed along the pier
they look good in the sunlight for a while
then they just submerge and drown, they're insincere
they rust and go insane
they rust and go insane

The murk as it cascades back into fluent light

illuminates the purpose of perhaps
beware the bridge is narrow
and they never wait all day
and worth it when they watch it all collapse

The mast on the water or a signet ring
an unlikely pattern we must choose
you close your eyes while sailing
and your craft collides with ice
the frozen north tears everything in two

Shelved sea collapses
it's an ornament
overflows, receding iron to your room
the water's rage by listless electricity
the pattern of armadas in the gloom.

HOW THIS ENDS

How This Ends (Part One)

HOW THIS ENDS

The blood flow moves like jagged ants
in the strobe of the conflicted sunset.
The markings on the face-clues, until they are smudged into
    hopeless graffiti.
The smoke seems to shadow its own mantra: How this ends.
In crying angels,
the sticks of the fire give up their ruined behaviour
in search of a climate closer to the amber of age.
The sun's tears spread persuasively onto bows
to help give voice to the coda.
How this ends
the observers lined up like Burnum
on the palisade rooftops,
no sense to be made of the city,
bridges span hours of rubble,
tenements, like swollen islands
stranded in molasses eyes,
the occupants burn linen and wood
in hopes of darkening the sky,
all anguish and empathy
detached and lining the riverbanks
like molten sentries.

Four men get out of a vehicle in cover of darkness

A crude skull spray painted on a toilet wall

Hopeless messages written in sand, destroyed by the tide.

A mountain of corroded motor parts piled on a former bird
    sanctuary.

How this ends:
in pictures, in a gallery,
in wall mounted mirrors
reflecting anxious throws of the dice, again and again.

The restless facades of doomed sculptures,
their attempts at realism swallowed up and mocked
by cracks in the floor.

Parades of birds peck at soggy canvases,
strands like anorexic worms hanging defeated and weak
from surly beaks.

The trains have slowed down to a glacial clip,
they bisect the landscape every couple of months or so.
The abandoned stations, mausoleums in the mist.
Timetables, white squares of zeros
wished under the fathoms
by spectrums of waving light.
Talk. Touch. Breathe.
There are bodies under the bridge,
flocking to the corners to hide,
the crescents of drastic light, two dog-skull eyes
on a landscape.
Shelter is pointless when the air brims with cremation smoke.

I'd remember the flowers,
but they are too easy to recollect,
how this ends: a million tangled stars surrendered at your feet,
their trails coaxing ice from molten cores.
I'd remember loves and numbered angels,
but they are far too easy to recall,

but I recall how this ends,
in whispered water,
too damn shallow to embrace with the mothering sigh you
    expected,
your nerves obliged to become crosshairs
while you patiently aim at airless shelves,
hiders of shadow and shallow movement,
the cryptic rustling deceptive as it ricochets off strange walls.
"How this ends"
they say, or ask.
Answers on parchment, too sun damaged to read,
the words caressed the page fondly before it died,
trying to change their meaning from inside so as not to offend.
How this ends.

Stained shells animated in the shadow of gables,
buildings bookended and praying to the city they lost.
Afraid of not drowning in the river,
afraid of not floating, ashen faced and freezing in the North Sea.
Stained shells, their innards bloated and slow
sucking at rocks on the headland,
hands reading them like clumsy Braille as we wait
for returning vessels, full of messages and memoirs.

How this ends.
Paradise.

The heavy curtains of a room billow slowly
like an upended sea,
seams interrupted by passive gusts from the outside edge,
soft darkness confused and silenced by air.
An army of full-length mirrors all competing for the one sliver of
    light
like fulgurite,
avoiding the bodies on the bed,

racked with disease and rage.

Tunnels of leaves
too frail to hide the body parts
something new:
more black than Picasso's blue
won't the birds shut up?
To salute
the killer's act of mercy
covered in leaves
eye socket or black cavity
as blemish becomes foliage
foliage into blemish
how this ends—tunnel of leaves
floodlight bloodhounds
runaway voices
with insane slogans
paintings of mules
alcohol in the abstract
worms in the fingers
worms in the fingers
wedding rings for psychopaths
birds' heads in black circle eyes
the colour of leaves mate with skin
taut with waxy terror
how this ends:
a discarded tool to the side of the head
how this ends:
a hasty raking to hide the shame
how this ends:
twitching under a carpet of chaos

Again.
How this ends.

Bleeding from the lips in lieu of happy birthday,
hands clutching at embers over candles.
White crosses in fields are just concussions,
the crossed eyes of startled insects
trying to stare and focus
as we play hide and seek in our bleached summer splendour.

How this ends
the ghosts flow out of the cupboards,
the cupboard doors slammed in unison,
a single handclap
for a single word,
washes of magnesium envy usher them out hastily
and children start to waken
dizzy with bipolar dreams
washed ugly by icy night sweats.

The heavy curtains of a room
drawn back sharply,
breath-taking and immediate,
highlighting the dust of powders and papers, money and wrappers,
the stubbornness of the clock's tick tock,
and the piano's seething silence.
Paintings of families, butchered by time
skewered on the metal hands of old station clocks,
skulls fractured by abandoned city cathedral bells,
swing, swinging, how this ends,
the room now alive with the ringing
and the ghosts of the once-rung.

The bodies stir on the bed,
touching down into the treachery of their surroundings,
the decision, the action, the lie,
cycled again and again
until there is a symmetry of scandals and curves,

the sleeping brave, their footsteps deadened by dense ashes on the
    floor,
smugly reflected by the drenched moss on the walls,
treading like feather soldiers around the room,
the heaving lungs of the curtains sighing a question
or a statement:
"how this ends"
wheezing and spluttering back into the blemish of night,
their crackling thoughts sucked through the anæmic slit of a
    window,
to have fingers of dim light pointed at them in mocking judgement:
"how this ends"
"how this ends"
and the train is filled with children,
running from one end to the other,
and the room is filled with children,
careering from one side to the other,
and the river is filled with children,
jostled angrily back and forth
by the movement of barges and bridges.

The city soul fades
the room just a pocket of air,
streets awash with zeal and venom,
clues as to the contents of the corroded,
vessels rolling slowly away from the docks,
leaking a yellow dismay,
all the sting without the honey,
all the dreams as dreadful as the patterns carved on your face,
the blood flow looks cartoonish in the ever-flashing light.
Accelerated to the speed of your final chapter of breathing.
How this ends.
How this ends.
How this ends.

The beauty of it seen from above
through chalk splinters and whirlwind lights
a meandering path of dull pink rocks stretched from
a tired and defeated peninsula
all the way out to a holy isle.

The abbey long disfigured
it's mottled stony bones
picked raw by these avian invaders

Ghost orchestras shadowed by the Pentland Firth's
icy overtures and fanfares
where waves bounce and reach up to the sky
hopes of copulating with the silence

And how this ends my sweet friends,
the last thing you see is the granite submerging
one after the other
like an entire book of last chapters.

DRAW A LINE.
PUT THE PEN DOWN.
GET UP AND WALK AWAY FROM THE TABLE

Being followed
to be followed
an exodus with the promise of roses at its conclusion
but followed, insolent eyes snickering and clandestine
a few miles further back.
Bodies under the bridge
trying to generate magic,
hopping and loping from rubble to dismal paradise,
post-war architecture, yellow stained,
cold and wet from piss and spilled solvents.
Sodium glare.

A stadium of pupils dilating.
How this ends,
flock to the edge,
iron palisades flank steaming canals of rank mater.
How this ends
lovers tweaked and teased apart by forceps
and stainless starkness.
A lip slowly moves itself against ice,
tries to form a prayer in the thaw.

You'd know it if you saw it,
you'd remember it if you heard it.
Cloying, begging, pleading animates the soul of saliva.
Brace yourself for the flowers,
the shadows of their stalks no different to the barbed wire traps
whose ground they share.

Fleeting gangs of the new innocent
picked out only by the dim orange light shafts
from tiny windows of embered kilns and mill houses.
Their tiny shrieks slapped hard against waiting walls.

To hear your voice when it isn't shaking.
To hold your hand when it isn't cold.
To close your eyes when you have not died of fright.
How this ends.
Try to pick yourself up from the slick ground
as you stumble to avoid the hail of poisoned birds.
Dead beaks and claws making meat of your milky eyes.
The brittle ghost of feathers licking you razor-raw
as you keep from falling and spilling.
How this ends?
Ignited air:
sheet lightning reveals tiny glimpses of laughter:
the upturned fur of frightened animals,

beaches of shiny secrets slowly loping towards the brine.
Fragments of wormy wooden figureheads
strewn beyond endless jetties,
their war-torn eyes humbled into watery holes.

No more islands
only silence.

Shanties, psalms and lullabies unsung at once like inverted bird
    calls.

A battle of blind hands on a church wall.

A modern era steeped in the heavy black ink of memory loss.

Four ghosts get out of a van and turn into statues.

Borders become lines blurred by millions of snakes.

Flowers martyred only by a truce between shadow and
to fall like rain on these islands,
to be the silence that interrupts silence,
and to slip quietly away
hiding tides from the mainland,
glory: a ring around the finger of a storm,
connecting the islands with an absence of light.
Glory—wildlife flee the islands
for a chance at immortality,
great swooping headwinds and waves
mop your brow and soothe you
after centuries of feverish worry.
and this is how this ends,
the whistle through eroded rocks,
urgent, mocking and insistent,
the chimneys of abandoned cottages

finally splinter in plumes of soot and shale,
seams of coal turn to slithery diamonds,
main roads give up on direction
and just point to the sea,
gulls leave their flocks,
in search of solitary air,
breaking like a heart instead of day,
you hear howls instead of seeing the first few rays of sun,
and you sing yourself lullabies in a loop,
trying to sleep through the gravity.

Your grainy, sliver eyes will not close,
the tight-lipped line of the horizon
interrupted by blisters of ruined architecture,
flecks of spit on a fading soldier's mouth,
wondering if this is how this ends,
the desperate last few patrician horses run,
shrieking, pell mell from the fire,
followed by hysterical birds and insects,
the sad bastards managed to put two and two together,
but the margin between prayer and the sea is just too narrow,
families no longer recognize each other,
and turn their faces down or away,
scurrying from the nest,
at different times, alone,
under cover of darkness,
how this ends,
you're gonnae have tae be brave, wee man,
don't come home,
stay under the twigs and the branches,
barely breathing,
walk slightly,
the mossy decay of corky bark under your soft hands,
walk, son
don't go home,

this is how this ends.
We have been dredging the wrong river for so long,
our black poles and nets angry score marks slashed across the
pig iron afternoon.
Slate sky plump with ready tears,
the bed strewn with useless wheels,
sodden engines,
leaking bottles and empty boxes of once genius design.
Where are you, sweetness?
Where is the note you said you wrote?
Are the words shattered, scattershot
across this silty path?
The curves of the c's
torn from the bars of the t's
trying hard to save the dots on the i's from drowning.

And you said you would write down how this ends,
about how I would collect comfort from the placid spaces between
    your remarks,
the soft white, underlined and ready for us to stretch upon.

Oh, how this ends!
Your words, fraying morsels
for predatory underbeasts
to pursue and gnaw upon.

The blank ink dilutes the sullen grey,
darkening again the tone of the river,
reversing again its mood,
the audience, if indeed an audience it is,
squatting mirthlessly on the embankment,
10-year olds with air pistols and rifles
wishing to cripple the circle of cawing
and screeching gulls that regale us.
Occasionally, a pellet or two will scald

us through our thick clothes,
and all we can do is wave our poles in the air with impotent rage.
Our voices raw to the bird's screeching caw.

Eventually, the day skulks off to an uneasy conclusion,
and we drift softly into an estuary,
hissing swans peck angrily at the quicksilver ropes
that try to submerge us,
pulling, weighted, freezing.

How this ends?
Do YOU know?

I had an amazing time of it
but now I have to go,
pining hard for a place I didn't really
belong to in the first place,
I shoo away the swans and gulls the best I can,
and take off my clothes,
diving into the inky water, shuddering and pulling myself down.

I'll find the words of your note by myself, letter by letter if I have to.

How This Ends (Part Two)

You must be kind enough to escalate
the fever that you want so
to project up every rope
that fell from hidden scaffolding
on gallows and on carousels collect,

A faintly cold anatomy that promises
the beaches that you hide on disappear
revealing nothing tangled
in survival slides

out of the sand it grew you—I'm glad the arctic threw you

A name so silent that it's beautiful
it curls around you and it's all to brief
it drops like seasons born with clouded etiquette
a stare that doesn't question your belief

Contraptions built by us and pushed along the pier
they look good in the sunlight for a while
then they just submerge and drown, they're insincere
they rust and go insane
they rust and go insane

A mask of friction hides the building door
they climbed so many flights to give you this
a murder, exhaustion, the flame beneath my feet
the stairwell and the virtue sorely missed

The murk as it cascades back into fluent light
illuminates the purpose of perhaps
beware the bridge is narrow
and they never wait all day
and worth it when they watch it all collapse

You must be kind enough
to leave me with my unrest
the Monday Tuesday of my thoughts
the fortnight of finales
traces back the curtain
reveals the stage on which we fought

You pushed us down the stairs
starved for the weekend
you gorged it whole, ate every part
you can't reach Saturday

reclusive in the shadows
on Friday, I keep saying
tt won't get dark

Shelved sea collapses
it's an ornament
overflows, receding iron to your room
the water's rage by listless electricity
the pattern of armadas in the gloom

The cold light cannot fight or evaporate,
the armies march from roof to cellar floor
intrusive-duties fall and trampled on the stairs
electric, as the sea conducts the shore

You must clime where paradise can't escalate,
a lifeless, airless edge to walk upon,
the damage, the crashes,
the fadeout on the roof
the drop will drag you gently 'til you're born

An avalanche of shrapnel changed geography
it burned what we knew about the town
they clawed their minds out shaking
and the clawing sounds they made
but the hill absorbed the injured
and their sounds

I could've hid by train tracks
where the horses stayed,
all engine battered stallion's limbless grave
the carriage soot survivors,
recorded them on tape
and played it back in churches where I prayed

The coal dust that I dug out from my arms and legs
a blood and powder tattoo of a key
you replicate in silver
it opens up the words
directions to our failures
and details

The mast on the water or a signet ring
an unlikely pattern we must choose
you close your eyes whilst sailing,
and your craft collides with ice
the frozen north tears everything in two

The sandstorm that we move amongst rids us of form,
no latitude, walls, floors on which to crawl,
it elongates all distance
shortens time to breathe
distorts the signals
chokes us when we call.

The painting's off the canvas
it's anonymous,
it used to guard the room in which we slept,
now dogs rip up the canvas like they're bandages
the paint looks like the wound from which it wept.

ARTIFICIAL MADNESS

Artificial Madness

On top of the hill
from every windowsill
who let them all talk
who let the birds never stop
I turn to my right
on the street artificial light
I run from my room
all the birds that have flown
they carry bits of my guilt
dot the sky like stab wounds

I'm here to deflate
the lights are warnings to celebrate
too tight to unwind
an artificial delinquent mind
afraid of the strain
when authorities call my name
I run to my street
clouds are raining deceit
they soak and cling to my skin
the flooded levels I'm in

Artificial madness
on the wish list of the frames you drew
make it mad but fake for fun
there's nothing more deranged to do

The city is blown
the good intentions were never known
too dark to divide

an artificialist paradise
careers of the heart
the madness atlas is blown apart
I run then I fly
invader of private sky
to fall and swoop over walls
to never answer the calls

On top of the hill
you see processions are never still
who let them all march?
Who brought them back to the start
incredibly dressed
the would-be soldiers that never rest
they run through the town
the flimsy buildings are falling down
they fake out and find
artificially mine

Wait for Amateur

If there's nothing else I need
I have nothing more to say
no more waiting for conclusions
while the reasons run away
and the place is full of air
it's a disease to dissent
or a palindrome of X
amateur dissident

Make a mark in the ground
with a primitive tool
now you never have to listen to the amateur rules
Wait for amateur, you've been waiting for an age
just like the Beckett play

on an amateur stage

When I shake a hand
I walk away in disgust
no more faking up the nice
no more fucking up trust
and I'm trying to be quiet
and I'm going to be nice
while I memorise mistakes
transgressions and vice

All the people on the ground
made inert by disease
dying slowly at night from the amateur freeze

Wait for amateur
or just turn and walk away
amateur player
in an amateur play

Classically Wounded

A whisper carved from passages of rain
blows past this age of off-key disdain
stop staring, stop caring
I can navigate a map without you
the streets are only bows without strings
and negative impressions of things
backed into a doorway
the vehicle of your dreams is on fire

Classically wounded-mysterious conductors hands
a series of somnambulance
the ambulance destroying our plans
the makers of emancipated glass refracts us light for light

every second of uncertainty
ascends and blurs conductors sight

The heavy-handed rooms are enclosed
the rooms without doors quietly imposed
so cruel, bejeweled
the great unanswered call has rung out
the choir eclipsed by riots and rage
undeveloped past the metaphor stage
consoling/controlling
the risk is built on friction and fright

Cold Blood in Present Company

Cold blood present tense
the more you look, the more intense
the fractured list of things to find
walking severed reaching blind

Dream blackmail perfect lie
hear the melody in battle cry
the cold blood of a dying bloom
sleep squandered in an empty room

Private war present company
a tense silence in front of me
precipitation and the price of pride
future perfect and the past contrite

The rain falls disguised as glass
the stained objects we never pass
remembered letters imagined notes
cold blood and surrendered quotes

The Modern Swine

I see it under the sand
the blinking ocean the blistered hand
I'm stopping only to look
don't want the photographs
that you took

And I'm climbing over the hill
the pressure lets me
the pressure will
and butchering the designs
to run away from the modern swine

You jump from wire to wire
the steeples buckle / brittle spires
and every ghost is a hoax
we'd like to speak
but we were never close

Wish I could trust you to spill
all of the wonder but you never will
it's going to find us in time
why run away from the modern swine

I'm telling it back to you

The fix is part of the flow
the fractured rivers
where we never go
we took our shame by surprise
a stunted lover
in a bad disguise

The fifth is eating the sixth

we're all survived by her dirty tricks
and secrets separate signs
hold a mirror to the modern swine

Imperfect Star

The doubters and the counsellors drop by
to risk their lives designing reasons why
the portraits and pretentions aren't enough
the stables burning down while we float up

The candy light contention drips away
the altruistic sarcasm will pray
the pirate prima donnas stare and stalk
the blood that flows discreetly never clots

Accounting to the martyrs
the system going pale
I'm waking up the storm watch as we sail
managed to save the surface from surprise
the risk is just redemption in disguise

A force fed freak of nature dressed in black
is blinding us in seconds turning back
the risk reveals / the damage falls in reels
the glancing blow to glances that we steal

The perfect figure eight imperfect star
who cares if it can light the way you are
you drown in clouds the whisper walks like wild
the measure of contrition is beguiled

The Paraffin Hearts

It's consistent / mighty cowards
cold and distant / but the work is done
parachute falls / parallel idols
I breathe on your neck / Sahara skin forever thin
you curl like a stranger / a manic glider
with half-the-way style

So much for applause
"speed" I shouted
silence stepped
a round of cruel stares
unwit the bride
she's off to the side
a place for the shapeless
a new kind of hurt
that smirks while you sleep
controlled and assaulted
the one hand clap
re-employed as a gunshot

The only way to tell us apart
you have to take a flame to our paraffin hearts
and whichever one decides to ignite
decadence won't make it right

I feel the heart shape and the muscle escapes
from airless age
just to turn the corner
to change the words
or turn the page

The Subjects

Never a beginner
you never took by force
and you couldn't break the skin
careless graph at the antic's source

The circuit of seclusion
the second joke is the law
and you read about removal
the perfect lie and the perfect flaw
(and you cast too far)

Pressure drops: revolving
they lie end to end
the same we said of circles
but they don't expand
I'm still a kid
and my answers stall
I could trade a stare for bullets
while the subjects fall

Money on the highway
smoking black exhaust
some countries never listen
no matter what the cost

And the hands are clawing wingless
upended angel flight
they only trawl across the grey
they only smoke at night
(and they cast too far)

The Goner

A miniscule asshole
winds up at a crack motel
then sent out to pasture
in fields where empires already fell
another fixates on guns
and tries to hide them, and digs and frowns
the hidden cargo corrupt
the powder ignites / your world erupts

To turn me on you're a goner/ a ggggg goner

You're not correct to control
clumsy fish in a stagnant pool
so no one listens to you
they stay submerged and seductive
to always act with your eyes
they're glazing over in paradise
and blinking Morse code at me
they stay submerged in misanthropy

You turn me on you're a goners / a ggggg goner
and when you stir up the questions
the hand grenades and the stun guns
you never reach a consensus
to fade in volunteer air

A Career in Falsehood

The certainty is savage
it wakes you up each day
to rake a brittle coast
or to sanctify the words you say
the folding of the letters

the framing of an outsize ghost
the sinking of salvation
you're getting far too close

Surprise will take a nosedive
from the roof of the banal
observed by swollen armies
from the bed of the canal
a counterpoint to candour
lifts the wet into a war
then you ridicule the answers
like the questions did before

Oh but I am nothing if I'm not weak
with a new career in falsehood as we speak
I lied my way through gravity and grace
then lied back to my likeness just in case

British Drug Lords

Afraid of gold
my story's never told
what was that sound?
My fever cooling down
well I learned to fool
just about everyone
never spoke the truth
always left the house alone

Contempt for clients
the stifled rhetoric
I work like science
to put these deals to bed
what would I do without no servitude?
I'd call on you

to milk your attitude

Moving more than you think
lookin' for a good cheap high

Looks and myths, I don't know anything
made myself up just for today
jump and stun my way into a runaway
hiding crimes in the city-wide shine
different colours / different lines
British drug lord time

Forced to the deck
the pictures and the text
reads like a list:
all adjectives dismissed
I'll clean my walls
chorus and obituary
when I leave my room
it's someone else's history

"I slow down, your world surrounds me
    like a cop you don't stop watching,
    phrase the question like an invitation
    to a past engagement
    garden parties dressed to kill
    with spy regalia
    lost your will to die"

Makeshift disguise
all my looks have just capsized
scrape it off the floor
dim the lights and lock the door
no one will see
mirror bent round the whole of me

mirror wings can't fly
just reflect off the wall to me

DAY OF KNOWLEDGE

Hotel Grozny

I'm the trailer of love through corridors
the dawn defying restless eye foreigner
the card in clenched fist
is a key with no matching address
the walker is moved by no feelings
of grief and distress

And meanwhile in the kitchen
the oddest of rituals takes place
a soft and low howling
smoke seen from the streets
the inside of the building
is hot and deceitful
while the flames conquer grandly
there is hardly a sound
and you can't ever see
the blind burns to the ground

The hard light through keyholes of boudoirs
project in a line of kino of cinescope
film loops forlornly
shapes you can just about wait for the smoke to stand still
the last secret wish
of Lillian Gish
blends into the face of some circus disgrace

And then a door opens
some broken down agent
wet cloth to his face
and he cannot see the exit

he is followed by a dame
in a "dance with me" evening gown
polished Barretta
lipstick illuminates
just part of the way

The banging of bedsprings
starts to ricochet hollow
against every wall there is a piteous uproar
no one knows if it's fists or illicit compassion
or a prize-winning gesture
of courage in the face of defeat

We are down in the bar
all the bottles are shattered
(the booze just evaporates)
or bursts into flames
reflecting off spangles
of glass on the floor
the light as it coruscates
off smoke and pianos
all broken songs sung
and the sheet music blackens
we wait for the chorus
but it's not going to happen

The ballroom, it levitates
all clouded from misfires
all roads-like veins voided
they lead us to here
eye shaped and empty
no dance, just collapsing
we are minus our grounding
and our atmosphere

Silhouette Lodging

Have you ever been apart
trapped underneath silhouette lodging
misguided powder light
the gasp for culture is cult of blame
the paintings slashed within its frame
the clocks don't chime unless it's out of spite
and the saints go bang bang
until they bite

We're not waiting, we're a ghost
trapped like designs in action paintings
who cares about your sculptures and your mediums?
Too bad the air is worthless
where our egos burn
I told you that I'm reason
the only one you have
the saints go bang bang bang
like they are above the law

Bones Interrupting Light

A secret made into a solvent
light falls off the endgame

You wake up and feel like you are falling
full swing hammer sullen sun
a bone thrown to amnesia
holy mist drenched water
the real beauty
as drops roll off drops
sea slides off sea
rivers run off rivers
the water is scarred

drowned by itself
choking in a life less secret
"communion X"
starved by alarm
the politics are playthings
left brittle by weather
rust replaces sand replaces emotion
ice neglects the sun
"communion X"
stamps logic on wildlife
crazed whispers
from the next world
bones interrupt light
bones
negative
flailing as such
"communion X"
ice neglects
"communion X"
ice neglects

Satsita One

The flight is bleeding
bleeding black from the clouds
red race in the air space
radar cloud sweeps over the mainland
the burst in the groin
Opposite of childbirth
TULA TULA TULA
Satsita
flight wasted in warzone
you'll find her up there
groin explodes in the air
wait here

wait to board
Moscow to nowhere: nowhere to Moscow
Satsita
velocity flames over killing fields
trajectory waves: as an orphaned hand
Tula tula tula
Toxic land scorched blacker still
you observe her descent
Russia to nothing
air space screams in bereavement
martyred fuel
belt to groin: hand to belt
Satsita
Who knows?
Holes buried in the atlas
use the weak light and teeth to I.D.

Satsita Two

Satsita
groin bursts sister first
too fast to hear
too fast to make a mark
twin flight paradise
Moscow to nowhere: nowhere to Moscow
TULA TULA TULA
Use the weak light to show the field
silence shines hard on metal
the opposite of childbirth
now boarding
black hole in air space
Satsita satsita satsita
groin explodes in mid air
holes burned in the mapless earth
OPPOSITE BIRTH ON TWISTED EARTH

AGENTS COMBING FOR I.D.
THE MOTION OF ALL OPPOSITES AT ONCE
SATSITA SATSITA

My desire to die is greater than your desire to live

Day of Knowledge

Day of knowledge
no words
no answers
and nature's hungry frame
invisible and clawing gently
at the between hours
a constant layer
and a fleeting lair
strips of the black sky
wrapped coarsely around servant's heads.

That which will puncture history
savagely thrust into gasping groins
the merest whisper of trainsspin tight lipped around the last
    painting

The charts of the skies have changed
slow moving vicious stars
willing towards bloody science
silent science
loping towards the day of knowledge
nothing beyond science and evil
zealous void
the opposite of reverence
do you drive in a car?
do you take the train?
the encrypted texts leave

a transparent clue
hanging above humanity

Ghost graffiti
diseased with double meanings
twin sisters smashed against
idiot walls
to suffer and decipher
hidden in plain sight
to step out of time
him over there
slightly lopsided gait
he suffered an injury at some point
maybe her? toying with her phone,
staring at it as if it might hatch
are you driving?
the van to your right, two cars down from a cop
the resigned compulsion
distant helicopters
lazily circle a change in history

Push it all aside
bang bang
quiet please
day of knowledge indeed
detonation by cowardice
disguised by fear
and night strip masks

You will not know us
because killing becomes anonymous
after a while
like sweeping up leaves or debris

The collective fear of an entire race

a grand thing to behold
it stands and grows
threatened tree of glass limbs
caved in face of a god
bad dreams the size of mountains
glass shards in jars
glass shards in jars
drifting balloons
drifting balloons
look for a hiding place
bleeding from the mouth
drifting balloons in the silent sky
drifting rifles
psychic etchings / slow motion graffiti
glass coiled like a spring
suspended above you
all we can hear is
the voltage turning on itself
the tribe's slow defiance
burns like an ice age
drifting from Caucasian lanes

Near Lethal Doses

Nights joined at the hip
in the final heat
ink cloud bursts
heavy with leaded shadows
toxic air sucking the piss from your mouth
foot stuck on the board
balloons drift away from the mountain sky
make slow their aimless escape
shadows of heavy flies
on the corpses
kolokol, kolokol, kolokol

the whispering of the stars
so brief the relief
arms struggle to the surface of the corpses
near lethal doses of heroin
near lethal doses of morphine
fight through the pain
sent by the struggling hands
kolokol kolokol kolokol
desire death more than you want life
shoot the ceiling
shoot the roof
drifting balloons in the silent sky
mother's arms dragged from dead child
drifting rifles
glass shards in jars
slipping slowly on sweating walls
the roof melts
near lethal dose
your passage will not be
frantic mask falls
heat mist traded for sleep
slow bars of shattered waste
stay still under the bodies
fat sluggish flies
boy soldiers war silence
are we not human because we believe in a cause?
foot on the wooden plank-don't move it
glass shards in jars
suspended at head height
women killed for revealing mercy
men left limbless to die
fear grows in strength from suffocation

You will not know us for our coward masks
near lethal doses of heroin

history is wretched
sent up in poisoned smoke
scream crescendos
broadcast in fragmented video
grainy voyeurs
shrouded conspiracy
safely repeated
behind bedroom doors
camera mask to foot
foot to mask
black wires suspended at head height
children's hands under corpses
gasping for disguised wretched air
not rebels
not freedom fighters
enemies of reason
blood burned to silence

The roof melts
near lethal dose
your passage will not be
twin sisters in paradise
limbs explode in the martyr room
detonated at the groin
shadow of mercy
on their faces
just seconds before
the apartment empty
the planes boarded
passage of time interrupted
actors thrown from the theatre stage
kolokol, kolokol, kolokol
whispering of stars
too brief for relief
axe sparks from trees

sucking piss from wet clothes
twin sisters obliterated
in the shadow of mercy
agonism
screams at crescendo
agonism
tiny balloons black dots against sky
agonism
glass shards in jars

Duty of Oblivion

The greed swivels
the constant is under fire
a scream to defend
defiance on a trip wire
awaken in ash where solemn animals pray
the duty to oblivion
decide where the embers stay

The scars stare and you're circling the waves
the punished impulse
the stillborn illuminates waste

We're wilderness in shiver shakes brighter
than the womb
with never-nerves disintegrate their splintered bones
all over the floor

Decline dawn's electric
we somehow shake and torture the still
its purpose to replace a fading crime scene
with a force of will

A pool of threatened thrown accidents in foreign climes

conditions they had worsened
the duty of oblivion is mine

Birth scars stare and you are circling the grace
circling the grace
the punished impulse
the stillborn illuminates waste

We're wilderness in shiver shakes brighter
than the womb
with never-nerves disintegrate their splintered bones
all over the floor

Once in the Water

Unless you have something to add to the list
a cast of surprises, a clutch of a cut of the wrist
a major step forward that made your remains
collect of a crowded town
it's just always the same

Once in the water always together
never to wander never to part
a ghost of contrition, a sand dune, a saviour
no more permission needed to start

A flight plan is forged with the aid of an aim
the close beams of silence kiss through the smoke
and the rage
the room is inside you it opens your gift
it's passed-over secrets all up in anger you felt

A hand curls around a significant heart
and squeezes it hard, it can never be blue
it drips jealous martyrs on rosaries red

makes your religion lift back to the stars

Congregation of Cruelty

Climbing slowly and furiously through rare forests
the trees, muscles of battle
frank in its judgement
splinters embedded in tongues
watch them dry
the birds flew away for the last time
when they discovered the carrion was toxic
some knackered horse; a death wish
a few drops of water snatched away from them
watch them dry
we were so close once before
dirge canals
dug in secret between austere plains
with nothing to fill them with
except flies and promises
catching the dust as it falls
and fossilizes like shale
onto molten roads
the sun is an army
not a thing of beauty
congregation of cruelty
stealing and scorching until parched skin falls
then a choking dust in bleach hot winds
we were so close once before

The Intent

Walk to the edge
didn't do it right
trouble in mind with a parasite
clean it fast

declare its litany
the guilt, it flies right back to me

Shot through wrist by glass and blade
soul for soul a blood exchange
don't cross yourself
in light of birth
clean it first
and search the earth
most of the time I'm through with it
not released or intuitive
'cos that drive got a death wish stare
no second chance
or final stare

Shot through heart
by force of fright
woke again
'couldn't get it right
I wise myself, I'm over lived
the killing secrets
I couldn't give

THE COLLAPSE OF ETHER

The Collapse of Ether

And that I don't like the smile
and that I don't like the walk
and that I don't like the soul
and that I don't like the look
and that I don't like the lover
and that I don't like the secrets
and that I don't like the lies
and that I don't like the sleeper
and that I don't like the waker
and that I don't like the feeling
and that I don't like the invitation

Walking away from the sub-zero, starting again
branches weighed down, slowly, dreadfully
pecked by birds and ignored
the labels attached to your belongings
a midnight stirring
in the layers beneath your rage

Fill every bottle with piss and vitriol
pour it on the icy headlands

Walking away from an aimless fiction
too tired to steal anything else

The burdened strategies
that end in the collapse of ether

And that I don't care if I'm ignored

Waking up dizzy
on an anonymous station platform
speed of light bullets
ricochet
off the abandoned sleepers

Waking up parched
by some displaced motorway
weeds and ruined drainage systems

The company of echoes
as you feel your way blind
down a semi-collapsed school corridor

The age of being born in a vacuum
your first breath is no breath
an environment
that takes you away
and turns you inside out
and takes you away

The slow trickle of hiding places
quickly dissolves
the cement outlet into the river covered in birdshit
21st century priest hole

Ambush held in front of another ambush

Bridge across the motorway
hurling bricks and bottles at army trucks

And I don't like the air of this battle

A burning church is just a burning church
a burning mosque is just a burning mosque

a burning synagogue is just a burning synagogue

And martyrs are not martyrs

A poisoned schoolgirl is just a poisoned schoolgirl
a missing son is just a missing son
an executed husband is just an executed husband

And martyrs are not martyrs

A sadist is a sadist

Shudder at the mosaic of information
a shattered world of disclosure
where limbs do not fit back on bodies
where fingers outnumber fingers
blood is measured in oceans
before it evaporates
the opposite of life and death
hangs heavy then falls from the former sky to explode
desperate stop-motion Skype
Mali-Somalia-Uzbekistan
Grozny-Ingushetia-Sudan-Ethiopia
refugees turned away at the gates
heroin exchanged for suitcase bombs

The collapse of ether
the company of echoes
rose tinted misanthropy
cut up and layered between slabs of white noise
the end of beauty
the end of recorded messages
the end of beauty

No such thing as martyrs

The end of beauty
the end of rhyme
as the cherished prayers tail off into smoky darkness
the usual graffiti
inert
until brought to life
by petrol bombs and glass

When you woke
were you sure it was the last time you'd see her?
Did your anger cloud her beauty thickly?
Too thickly with miasma
did you bite your tongue
and tiptoe out so she would not wake?

The collapse of ether
the company of echoes
lifeless tracing of fingers
on drowsy maps

And I don't like the distance
all at once numbers, arbitrary
collide in the ether
to generate
the formulas of our undoing
naked flames
and blood cycles
people masked in the heat
genderless
mirage of arms legs and guns
and I don't like that you do not love me
speech aberrations
facial tics
random text messages
and I don't like the flow

final texts
skiped snuff
outline of a man, barely in your peripheral
the emerging mould of your undoing
Sudan, Sudan
wars hidden under the shadows of the modern
refugees colliding with borders
only to shatter and spray
and what the fuck do you want from us???
Uncontaminated water?
The collapse of ether?
The company of echoes?
Lock the borders
stamp systematically until extinct
you call it peacekeeping
we call it genocide
or the company of echoes
echoes of Stalin
rippled from a bloodthirsty maw
and that I don't like the water
and that I don't like the cold
the mercy of it is only knee deep
and you wake with the screeching flight
of every car bomb at once
a forest of twisted metal and prejudice
rogue wires, charred snakes on the road
where trembles time

Minutes quake where cities break
the long fall down
ground never gets closer
and we ache
for a world of disclosure
deep tunnels pried open
by force of truth

the virus in the infrastructure
the light exposes the worst in us
the poison in the water
sending the girls home
the long fall down
never gets closer
knee deep in freezing water
time trembles
waking rage
crushing hesitation
shot and dumped in clandestine locales
outside the city
or in abandoned buildings
salo re-enacted in the 2000s
by ultra-sadists
all fours on the shattered glass floor
world of disclosure
mosaic information
scraped from the darkest corners
spewing forth grid references
that end in subway disasters
and airborne holocausts
the long, long fall down
purged for days, then executed
the opposite of life and death
hangs heavy and from the former sky to explode
the worst in us
twitching limbs on the scorched ground
blood stabbed, post exsanguination
blood stabbed
lapped up by rats
and stabbed again
desperate stop motion Skype
teenage soldiers raped and sent out to rape in a wasteland
like the collapse of ether.

DECIBELS FROM HEART

Mistreated and Wild

West of the faithless, among the collapsed
the beauty of sunbursts, our hands overcast,
creating a causeway, from acres of text,
it rhymes with the right way, it loves nothing less

Caring for nothing, but a kiss from the past,
the lips fill a journal, so naked and fast,
current eyes revive rumours of yearning,
in this sky where the darkness is turning

West of the way we were
with thoughts that were never there
I'm starting to pour down
mistreated and wild
to a place built on connections to denial

Fearing the practise of long afternoons
spent hiding from ages, white wine and perfume
a cluster of hushed gasps, sweet air from your lips
wet skin from communion and off it we slip

Knowledge of rapture is all that I have
reviving the secrets that grow in my path
rivers drown but can't keep me from writing
verse of breathless age, verse of inviting

At Least When I'm Gone

Minus every time
too blind to look at me

and fell on every feeling
fall broken fantasy
she's the worst of every dawn
revealed unknown
a flame in saddest eyes
reflect and rise

At least when I'm gone, you're certain, you're certain
a fortune of grace goes to waste
we'll climb behind time
and become the deceivers
still raising myself and I'm hurting, I'm hurting

Swing every romance
with thoughts of an unlit sea
and perish every untruth
in desert history
afraid of every flow
disgraced by words
all language without worth
in time's design

Be Mine When You're Not Mine

It's totally backwards,
limitations and malaise,
from streets of sanguine stories,
a deified craze,
you're likely to ignore me,
too unified a thought,
you write your sanguine story
with shades of us you caught

I promised you a purpose:
be mine when you're not mine

my lover on the surface
just shine when you don't shine

Be mine when you're not being reflected
with scores of windows left over light
it's strange to me you're not being projected
where midnight screen adorers unite

A cardiac conspiracy
hides blood on crimson masks
from the risky womb of rhetoric
my lover won't react
she whispers holes like petals
her myriad mystiques
the silhouettes they settled
to suffer in deceit

I can't explain it clearly
be mine when you're not mine
you don't need to be near me
just shine when you don't shine

Cinema Thing

Whistle through familiar tenements
AM after 4 just echoes more
you claim your distance hungrily in staggered steps
the misty fiction air
obscures the door

The way you edit dreams creates afflicted truth
they move from scene to scene with borrowed shine
you leap from murky surface to a mirrored pool
you soak your silhouette and then soak mine

Will these sights continue to be loaded?
These blades of mercy qualify your name
a blazing shadow dips from coasts of secrecy
immediately paints you out the frame

First glimpse at a lasting lie sensation
assured by us the witness disappears
a maze of stifled love reluctantly replies
the whisper and the wondering so near

The middle of a cinema thing that sings

Decibels from Heart

Three questions leaked from
this dangerous heat to arctic rooms
the modern whispered
and caresses encrypted by the moon
distorted scent
of this woman's compassion beneath the sheets
while florid endgames
suck dry the will of poems by deceit

I would not pause
but this parody of perfume soaks the page
stray maybe the bullets
but I'm not afraid to tell it or engage
my darling fixture
you're the cause of second nature and surprise
the modern fracture
and the hole in which you disappeared inside

Breathe the broken air
while the things that keep it simple
curl the outlines of the pages

that you fanned upon the flames
stain the broken glass
then remove it from your palaces
the sharpness carving memories
the clarity collapsed

Lavender City

Lavender city
nothing to do
got to keep searching
for someone who knew you
maybe a picture
maybe your touch
and I walk by this river
for months and for months
a map of the alleys
but the alleys are blind
lavender city
it used to be mine

God, so much sunlight
but the buildings are dark
in lavender city, I'm back to the start
the parks that possessed you
boulevards that embraced
they wrote you a romance
and laid it to waste
in lavender city, the days of the week
used to kiss us with splendour
now they're dead in the street

Let's Be Actors

I was waiting,
west of the sun,
in the ghost lights,
shining as one
cowering, free falling
mystery's age
shades adagio, never been played

Introducing
scenes from the heart
with the curtains
refusing to part
let's be actors
play for a few,
write my own speech,
act it for you

Costume and covert
lay down with the lions
they breed amongst someone's disguise
I'll stare at someone
a sacrificed passion
code before class, peace at last

In a lifetime
learning your lines
saints of endless acts
wasting your time
bring your face down
close to the stage
you're a scene that's never been played

I was waiting

scared in the wings
shores of darkness
the audience brings
let's be actors
learn you by heart
if you learn me
right from the start

Workin' Time

I'm still inside, it's workin' time
you picked this time to leave us,
through misty gates, wet morning slates
the lover's lore between us
a horse and cart takes us nowhere
its silly hooves and wheels on smoky path
and when we hide the new year
takes its weight in wonder,
lover, workin' time
digs past the world for you,
oh lover, workin' time

I forged some papers, got a perfect score
and when I fly, you'll miss me,
I'll fall so deep, and I never sleep
through covered eyes you kiss me,
it's workin' time in this stillness
sail with open heart but my hands can't move
reach out to drain the first rain
slate covered whisper, oh lover workin' time
rewrites the end for you, oh lover
workin' time

To Swing from The Air

Though we tried,
we'll never fly
we'll swing from the air
things look so good from there
the palace and the wine
we'll never mention time

The last of chance
through mirrored stars we dance
depending when you're sure
the darkest mood azure
connected by our flaws
a love that never was

If we rely on our share
of swinging from the air
like love there's no one there
and we surrounded certain
with our shades of hope
whisper there's no one there

Secret flight
we'll never make it right
love behind a door
we can't open no more
the frantic and the serene
the one place we have been

I tell you what
two lovers left in shock
we'll swing forward and crash
too dark to know we're too fast
we'll fall and dance from this height

an irreversible night

2GloryB

To glory be and all of her histories
I wish to mention out her name
the way we're walkin'
candles over forests
the city's staged,
reach out to me

I'm passed across
by perfumed icons that we lost
too much to carry on the way
and we must pass this
a decade's own revolving zone
always so much more when we don't save

I won't second guess or even dignify the rest
can't even see, but glory be
the mirror in the darkest room
reflects but love and never light
cannot even see but glory be

The place is dry
just look at how we never died
I ran out calling for your name
it shakes and wonders
if we can't see, then glory be
you might just love me all the same

Your letters race in circles round an empty room
they represent as ghosts of leaves
a punished echo, the writing is illegible
the version, too much glory to believe

JACKIETOWN DEMOS

Jackietown

Mist in the well-cut night
his usual haunts obscured by fable
the stories told designed as lullabies
the beer and notebooks on the bar table

I turned myself into a man of the sea
'cos home is where it's hardest
the isolation borne in tunnels of hail
still wandering the farthest

A trail of murdered prayers
interrupts the Glasgow skyline
lifeline threaded through the closed door of a church
like a map to disappear my time

Feels like I'm crawling out of love
just to face the perfect danger
survivor's guilt inside the trust I built
all the motion becomes estranged

Jackietown, I miss the sound
the whispered wish into wandering daylight
the brilliant still cascades down endless hills
flood streets of Jackietown
with all his wandering daylight

You climbed the steeple first
up to the weathervane, and I watched
you fell like the words of a love song
to a fictional muse you lost

Carried my love through Jackietown
and we was stranded in the rain
and I was forced to remember the dissonance and the shame

A trail of morbid christs
through a maze of human sin
all the windows are cracked from heat
where does Jackietown begin?

The painting stripped of life and grace
just to make room for a faded message
read by none other in centuries hence
Jackie walks the darkest passage

The Last Renoir (A Fiction)

The last Renoir
is hanging by a wire
too scared to fall
too weak to climb higher

The muse in light
radiant in frame
skin like heaven
hair like flame

Two hands in a darkened room
etched in crystal by the moon

The branches blurred
as they navigate the sky
controlled by painted gods
without sun they'd rather die
she curves like painted mist

settles on the man
creates the blessed air
by waving slow her hand

Two hands in a darkened room
etched in crystal by the moon

ART AND GENDER

A Distant Black Spring

Hermes couldn't put it better
when he broke the seal with knives and paper
lifted from the gods
another confidence trick
to ruminate within.

Rivers stale within a waiting world
the sun slipped by unnoticed
'til we all but breathe a darkness
lifted nightly from the gods
another sleight of hand
with no apparent outcome.

Do we levitate with mercy
beyond a distant black spring?
coiled serpent on your desert
poised to poison all our literature
love stories into blurry smudges
rendezvous on frigid tundra.

And we whispered through our carriage window
to stations of the fraught
no coiling smoke or distance
or the outcome that we thought
just reverse impressions
strewn across a desert
to the wilderness of spring that we begin.

Signs, striation, boulder rubble
no sensation of a miracle

to mend a poisoned hand
see it slither down a hole
through the wormwood
past an estuary
our desert might turn sanguine
black corrupts like staged redemption
I realized my veins are almost empty.

A distant black spring
on its side, 'til it's past circular
its shadow flounces
in the braille of sand in air
cloth to stare through
at a staged eclipse
frail stars for us to read by
but it's thirsty navigation
throws its distance ever since
be the etching that you wanted,
be the cave wall you are thrust upon
I'm the constant: your amnesia
the hair you tug so strangely
oval mouths exclaim disdain
party moves from church to badlands
a life's work in a single water colour
slammed into a book.

People Become Estranged

People become estranged,
that's what they do
climbing on top of things
to wave goodbye to

People become estranged
they look away

just passing by you in the dark
to wave goodbye to

A lurking former lover
in her loneliness
fallout from a Pinter play,
a cloying former colleague
in clandestine acts
(with nothing new to say)
a nightly peeping neighbour
in the naked light
(taking pictures every day)

Union Canal Blues

I came down slowly
and I put out the light
you were wishing out fearless
as it swam from a fright
my soul is submerged
in the union canal
drowned by hounded graffiti
and vagrant dogs

I've got Union Canal blues

A tightly held scar
in the palm of the town
its blood never moving
but it never slows down
you breathe in the bridges
and I'm coughing up fuel
love on desolate barges
with never known gods

I've got Union Canal blues

Slim Volume

And I'm tearing away,
slim volume of poetry,
and I'm serving a sun,
illuminates what fear has done,
to my face, and my passage
to the history books you destroyed,
I'm a carving exposed to the ice,
just a wire worn in paradise,
won't you look at me now?
Grace frowns upon ya,
when you level your heart
leveled eyes, big city fires,
coronas, kingdom of cranial pain
seven dreams I had before the week had passed
seven reasons, seven lies
slim volume of instruction
introduced to the way it works

Carried back
too weak of spine
the roses are replacements
may the gold leaf shine,
may the words submerge
in their own disturbing statements

Too far south of a haven
removed from stark affairs
these carved ice slogans
deliver, but just for a moment
melt and the meaning is lost
that wire I said I wore?

Looks like it vanished
before I got there
and won't you look at me?
Leveled eyes
seven lies
Lasdun's slim volumes
and I'm tearin' away
use a blade to disguise my face
Ooooh! Ooooh! Ooooh! Ooooh!

Seven Days, Seven Lies, Seven Lovers

To climb in your direction
no method, no motion
hidden stains
behind my lover's page,
we graduate to beauty
from our toying with the tide
all in seven days, seven lovers

Painting masks on forgers,
to limit lessons that we faked,
outside the seven lies
surround your palace,
aim,
fire.

Seven lovers, no other
peephole view by hidded lantern
behind my lover's love,
precious skin
to the arid stare of your paper
back at me
before the swathe of the charcoal
seven lies, seven days

drawn at a table and left there,
to climb in your direction
the gorgeous charcoal curve,
writing lies, days, lovers

Art & Gender

When the deluge hit the street
it left shelter for the painting
it reflected every drop
burned like acid through the canvas

Oh, I never was a painter
but I could always draw my blood
and my deluge loves disaster
a fleeting triptych on the flood

I mistook horizons
then, in an arc I shook my brush
I tried to disguise every brush stroke
imposter of art you trust

Got hung up on art and gender
made for a wicked task
all those etchings, all those still lives
borne of vanished sex

Oh, I never was a writer
but I could always write you off
see my gender as pretender
oh, why can't I be both?

Pull the curtains back to reveal
the "life model" stance
you're becoming a slave to your sculpture

decide where to place your hands

Mama Bluebell

Mama Bluebell
you're licking your wounds by yourself
in the mirror
your shuddering eyes
mist too late

Mama Bluebell
you spoke belief
until we drained you
your cloak sent smoke
fell down, revealed you slick on the floor

Mama Bluebell
you're paralyzed,
the ground beneath you
will never rise
you get a feel for it
you get a feel for it

I'm out hunting
just scraping my ace
through your wasteland
and I shout "pow pow!" just to see ya fall
"pow pow!" at the end of it all
'Mama Bluebell

Stampede Weather

Close knit animals
all with midnight will
crossing over to

find a greater sky
and your point of view
burns the best of you
trail blaze stampede weather
I thought I'd never arrive

When the blood migrates
to a different place
there's a chill outside
where the hoof prints hide
the whole prairie sinks
to unmentioned depths
looks like stampede weather
I thought you'd never arrive

Saint Symptom's Day

Costumes worn betray
it's Saint Symptom's day
a message on your door, nothing more
you twist the meaning
'til it creeps through your window
and I say "you got it"
just stick 'em on it
I'll forsake it today

Great mercy, about time
you're just the last in a long line
and your hidden image and impromptu hair
makes it easy for you to get scarce when you're there

Shrink the sign of the cross
to a pin prick
is it worth all the times that you lie?
It's so easy to hide it's simplistic

for these onlookers
they never ask why

Great mercy, about time
you're just the last in a long line
and your hidden image and impromptu hair
makes it easy for you to get scarce when you're there

Old Hymn of New Intent

Will this mouth exposed
produce a prayer less listed to
more felt upon your soaring skin
will this mouth exposed
produce direction loud enough
to guide me from
a clustered darkness
to a fading desert
dressed for winter
dressed for occasions
such as the birth of an army
fading frequency
straying from the path of battle
boots march to gouge a mass grave
an old hymn of new intent
climbing fast signals
on its spider wires
to dream of messengers
garbled but still audible
ransacking a moment of memory…

FURTHER DAYS

That Angel Skill

The climate of love
before light from the never above
drives its drained destiny
a swarm that leads to the sea
a light that can't find you and me

It's pressed between books
a letter that dares you to look
blends its script with a clue
a list of the things you should do
glass shadows you are trying to look through

Few decisions beat that angel skill
can I not persuade you?
you're never too afraid to
light up the ghost inside you
I was hoping there'd be room to fall
but the walls are sacred
the air you breathe is wasted
like nothing you have tasted

I'll meet you and talk
find a way off this rock
but I'll weep when I swim
let the water get in
you can't drown without sin
I'm stoned and I'm frail
maybe blind, but I'm setting sail
just a world without land
a desert with shame for sand

in the still of my hand

THE TIDE STRIPPED BARE

Another Song About A Painting

Another song about a painting
wish I could have seen the first stroke
the bottle pouring sun in the chalices and glasses
and god came alive in the smoke

The pattern through the birches, a whisper
as silent as the river is wide
wait 'til the paint is dry 'til you kiss her
then throw your brushes into the tide

I miss her dance on canvas walls
the tallow lamps where shadows fall
from robes that levitate from land
the glistened eye, the shining hand

You never take your eyes off that island
it's weightless in the estuary
its movement a prayer to the greens and blacks
committed to its history

The lovers are discovered embracing
in every field where you ever walked
they're forced to run for miles in the waning sun
until the mist fatigues, and it stops

Heart Full of Clouds/Cloud Full of Hearts

At one point
still downstream
sometimes a sliver of sainthood

marked more than you can stare out
a cloud full of hearts

Unrested
from scraping the best of your love
why solve the mist of the endgame
the bringers of rain
just clouding your heart

And if you see me
don't follow me
cloud full of hearts
know what I'm thinking?
You win again
cloud full of hearts
want my prediction?
Without encryption
we have to make it work
before the thunder gets too loud
heart full of clouds

I'm walking
walls between sunsets
hidden chambers of instinct
rise silent
to altitude's heart full of clouds

Don't stop me
don't stop me from treading these walls
in time I'll trip on my history
the clouds, they will miss me
the bringer of hearts

Fickle Will

The missing will is fickle will
it glides to where the smoke is still
mosaic lights through forest eyes
no sense of shelter

When the gun is smoking
the mercenaries hoping
you're an angel not imagined or unseen

The street of folly occupied
some people never satisfied
they leave en masse, untraceable
no ghost seduced you

When you lie there waiting
your breath is hesitating
and it freezes in mid-air and disappears

New Omen

Found some new omens in a dream last night
walked shallow borders
sleep just didn't feel right
into the wishing well
dropped my clairvoyance
into the wishing well
and kept my silence

Found some new omens near a wounded bird
tree shadow trident
where the wind disturbed
I kept my counsel
but I lost my faith

and these new omens gone
without a trace

Much of this is angel stolen undelivered
much of this is wound descending
message lost
you find
you go
you stop
you know
new omen light

I drag my worthless wonder between two trees
and dug a hole through nightshade
watched the omens freeze
all speech is interrupted
by a glancing blow
all meaning is reversed
by truth we know

Found some new omens
when I turned my back
a field of covered eyes
by deserted tracks
I feel these distant sounds
like a pit of thorns
new omens disappeared
before I was born

Someone Else's Rope

I'm sick of these numbers
trying to count the strays away
and all these making assumptions
when it's never light enough to play

the mood just died: don't sentimentalize the "why"
it's your close-up stroke
the end of someone else's rope

And I'm out of focus
just a blur upon your screen
someone else's misread script
in someone else's dream

Bliss that traces outlines
I know you'll come around
it's the bell you ring from someone else's rope
sound shades another world

I'm climbing with heat
I guess I'll meet you near the sun
afraid of inverted stares
re-enter blind to carry on
the out-turned ride
the blame of reason in disguise
you never drown when you swim through mist
the end of someone else's list
a man out of literature
the face of someone else's tale
a fiction of distant risks
dirt under someone else's nails

The Blue Fraud

The bliss is out of context
fire thinks it needs a warning
we bluff our way through thoroughfares
to be there in the morning

Hazy lights on bridges

the blue fraud underwater
so hastily we jump to save
the certainty we sought

And the night was in a coma
as it forced me to repeat you
like a mantra in a car crash
a disaster you can sleep through

Stick around; these flames mean nothing
they can't even squander air
but they burn into your memory
the blue fraud in the distance

Quietly hide from the blue fraud on my back
when these prayer words are dust on my tracks
I want to move you badly
to a truth you never knew
can't compare
to my fraudulent blue

Forgotten in sedation
the smoke will work around us
while we trawl these hotel hallways
trying to catch the blue fraud

You collapsed into its verses
'cos it will not leave a clue
and the signal it reverses
like surrender over you

And the night was in a coma
so it couldn't hear your urgency
like lust into a void
slow motion into mercy

The blue fraud on the staircase
movie-glides onto the esplanade
and cut to fit the memory
the light just failed

The Tide Stripped Bare

To follow you there was uncertain
the person I dreamed of becoming
lost in shade of footprints
the distance
collects like sand in a jar

I'm climbing and wading in still-time
it's still mine, the frame 'round the canvas
is air that escaped from a bell jar
it's too far
it falls like sand from a star

I'm driving the tide like a psychic
it won't move, it's stuck before orbit
it never begins to unshore me
before me
disrobes like the water to wane

Light clawing its way to a surface
your surface, its roots in the darkness to come
it begins to control me
disown me
the tide stripped bare of the sun

Don't disturb me while I'm waiting for the tide to strip bare
stand a lifetime in this ankle-deep affair
run the current while I rest between the cries of your crests
while the stars are bleeding sand, the tide remains unimpressed

A thing we could do is to leave here
in secret, two dots shrinking back on the beach
while the camera finds us
defines us
a mark for a place in your book

These words can't hope to explore you
before you slip from the rocks at the cliff
to place you're sacred, wasted
a mark for a place in your heart

A cry you lost in the passage
the message, I'll leave if you want me to leave
not as if I was born here, belong here
a sign for the thing you can't find

The tide stripped bare as it cleanses
it sends us the words to redeem or reduce
anything we could witness, we'll fix this
the tide stripped bare of its air

Ophelia Moment

Oh for the sake of landmines
the golden hair entwined
drop the rays of aimless sun
onto a demigod

That icons hardly listen
drips from a diamond avatar
transparent in betrayal

To the moon I offer silence
to a voice no longer literate

these thrones too deep with poems
(and the waiting, and the wading)

Ophelia
long shadow movement of water
there is no worse day
desperate air
hidden by the flustered leaf shadow
shallow flame
buried shallow
a moment
a feather scrapes the earth
time and again
Ophelia
your mad shadow
posed like a question
slaughtered like a mannequin
conduct sweetness to earth
heaven sweetness to earth
easter clandestine
and I'm beginning to see a repeat
and I'm beginning to see a repeat
and I'm beginning to see a repeat
and I'm beginning to see a repeat
poised like a question
or a figure: prone
Ophelia
conduct your sweetness to earth.

I'll leave you yearning for another day
long drinks and whispers on the lawn
you'll be my baby bathed in funhouse grey
so pale and slender, as a fawn.

BLOODHOUNDS

Bloodhounds

Was it despair?
Was it a sudden scare?
You don't need light or life
to find the bloodhounds

You weren't there
but I could feel your air
you don't need a sense of crime
to find the bloodhounds

And you were wrong
because we found the forest gone
no sense in anyone trying
to hide from bloodhounds

The mantle draped
over such sanguine shapes
lick from the hunter's bowl
it's just the bloodhounds

Look at the trails
just like the way I failed
you don't need compromise
to find the bloodhounds

You melt with shame
just as the headland drains
the sky is crossfire
it can't touch the bloodhounds

The sky well fed
from all the blood we shed
we'll bleed alone all night
right beside the bloodhounds

Jump, Goddess, Jump

Come back to me, I never see
the way that love can pray for pain
these signs of life
dividing knife
and love cannot reflect the same

Look past the time
this love is crime
held by its throat against a wall
leaving your thunder
your unmet voice
to drown out words
before they call

Making the time
to divide the source
slippin' away from the stunt
we can hope
to jump goddess jump
look at designs
we decide
to not cover the front
and we shout from the back
to jump goddess jump

How crude the fraud
how could we not
I'm passing love my speed exhales

stunt double eyes
for certain rise
jump goddess jump
before we fail

We climb inside
a paradise
we forged
from staring down our loss
building it back
from last attack
where love
cannot reflect the cost.

Ascension

And I blame it on the ice
that made the ground too hard to breach
and it didn't stop the maze of branches
in the winter light
too hard! Too complex of you!!
Moving monastic
a prayer lost in Saint Catherine's shadow
a cliff-hanger ending
and an upward shift

And she was martyred in a motion
the secret sound of angel's wings
she stands alone at her ascension
waits for the bells that never ring

Connect saliva to the dots of feral blood
again, the bloodhounds
gorging on a ghost
the scene in woodcuts

abandoned on the priory floor
the hissing windows
cannot deflect the cold

I see a solace near the floodlights
there's something rustling in the dark!
Too quiet and hesitant for footsteps
transparent Catherine and her spark.

A Farewell to Athens

A farewell to Athens
and he said he wouldn't quit
he's been lying here since the 1980s
he is so out of reach of his heart
just toying with the blood flow
as his story disappears
do I have to say goodbye? It's so noisy
seems like the streets will never hear
they'll just carry on dissolving
while he pretends he's lost his language
too barren for words
he just hovers over silence

I can feel a crisis line
the coast beat by my truth.
The mist hasn't been here for ages
and I never searched for clarity
I'm glad that you muddied my water
now I never have to say goodbye

A farewell to Athens
he's blacked out on Calton Hill
he's been lying to you since 1982
the black circumference of heart

not a plaything, nor an enigma
just the inverse of birth
he takes a willing stab
to blueprints of Atlantic
another blind man in the firth
just modeled after a whispered road—"I'll only take me home
    again"
Black Hill transmissions
of cremated heart: it's Athens in the dark

The mist hasn't been here for ages
and I never searched for clarity
and I'm so glad you muddied my water
now I never have to say goodbye

Anna Karina's Guide to Being Mesmerized

Each second the mercury
falls inside of me
shines like alchemy
falls in love with me
turns it's back on me
somehow mesmerized
mercury baptized

You could have been her
my Anna Karina
lofty esteems glaze those tenement eyes
creeps past the night
l'escalier dies
instead of her shadow
left us mesmerized

And she's still complicit
with the love of your life

a light shines obliquely
on the films she's inside
belle at the table
during Chinese roulette
dazed and delinquent
is what you will get
we climb over lovers we wish we could taste
Karina's silk curtains
and hypnotized lace

Encyclopedia of Haunted Lovers

Come here forever
my stained little angel
our fevered pollen
keeps us in the dark

Stars skate away like bridesmaids
from all the shotgun weddings
the bloodshed on the bandstand
in the park

Love hunts us
and the bloodhounds
will detect us from our nosebleeds
the air up here too thin
to suffer fools

So we inch by vine from cirrus
to a window you left open
and a badly planned escape
the time is cruel

My skill is in the friction
of my flesh against an apparition

clear blood
through the climax of a stare
when love is just a fiction
a fable you can die within
the perfect romance
nobody is there

Come here for certain
my stranger to the angels
my words will not be doubled or defined
that words drip from a comb
and lie like lust and brevity
the paper wings transparent
and inclined

We double bluffed the bloodhounds
drug sniffers at our ankles
but our triumph must be hidden
from the hunt

My baby, you're a drifter
shake treason from your powdered wings
statue still was never what you want

Our Last Conversation

Are you missing something here my dear?
Any closer to collect?
Those doctors at twilight
so needlessly intrude
the bodies and the instruments reject

We miss our breathing space
our time to fly
our messed-up version of goodbye

our safety somehow trapped
on a sun blind map of firsts
our messed-up version is denied

Your quotes, like markers on a riverbed
between ophelias and rust
you drift by proxy
and you drown by dream
and it's the only death you trust

We miss our breathing space
our time to fly
our messed-up version of goodbye
our safety somehow trapped
on a sun blind map of firsts
our messed-up version is denied

We miss our breathing space and our reflections,
the chrome all wasted in the sun
but rust bleeds beauty into heart shaped novas
the twilight vector s almost done
please be a secret keeper!!
Please don't make us notice
that shadows pulled from under us are ghosts
not your trial
it's your bereavement
that tightens weary eyes,
climbs back from you,
and frightens us the most
we miss our shallow rivers,
our lovers, and our shivers,
that sting of fright that warms us back to life.
come down with me, my honey,
drop solace on your magnet pearls
and be with me

we'll barely breathe tonight.

I Figured It Would Be My Undoing

When I walked here with you
hidden voice, lens, and talking about you,
card arrived, still survived
no location, no invitation too...

Now I'm thinking, you're insisting
a way of moving, my undoing

And we sing, oh, oh!
Never pass a waste of sunlight
I never tried to do right
I figured my undoing now

And the crowd spilled a tear,
no regrets, babe, just get me out of here!
Shots the size of my heart
ring like frenzy
they pull us all apart

Is it curtains? Just be certain,
I'm still proving, my undoing...

I Dream in Argentina

I dream in Argentina tonight
the light of rain and purpose through my room
a full length mirror
and a dancer's escape
we're fortunate to know you
and your feverish talk
I dream in Argentina

and it's locked

I dream in Argentina all my life
the same wish that a different language might
Camila's ghostly outline
projected on the plaza walls
and I dreamed in Argentina
while the other dream falls

The quiet family seen leaving
through elevator doors
concertina shape shade
on the children's facade
they glide slow on the flagstones
while they bow their heads
they dream in Argentina instead

I dream in spinning wheels
and the lights of Linda
her mercy is undressing
on the wooden floors in sunlight
her amethyst passage
in a straight-line walks
her stride ignites the flagstones.
She never dreams
she never talks.

Richter Grey Stairs

Stairs slide in front of my eyes
I fall, risking the mist
I timed this evening
masts of paper indoors
reads under the poems
without believing

Conflict: the page falls face down
the crossed arms send signals to winter
maps of envy: inverted
close pathways in the dark to the centre

Life ain't like the lion's share
it puts all your whispers to bed
stares in disguise
to big to hide behind these monochrome eyes
keeps on watching your progress
too slow
on those
Richter grey stairs

Mirador, Matador, Minotaur

And will something come in
to the sun barren room
cover holes with an eyeless intent

The thread lies forever
but it blends to the floor
a visionless compass is spent

My fever is coastal
it sticks out my soul
like a grave in the sand

And will someone use pigment
graffiti indignant
but the message on walls is too old

Thread maybe endless
wound tight pattern senseless
matador minotaur sold

Another Song About A Sculpture

Another song about a sculpture
it eats me just to be in here
gallery eyes from a luminous drain
mission sucked from another year

The scale of reason irrelevant
translated like you're viewing time
its fathomless width seen from under the door
the darkness of the room defined

Tide stripped bare of its waning
survivors of a curious flood
beach dynamic on the head of a pin
deluge of an artist's sun

I can't get used to this system
the building, then the taking away
the flow of the media too late to concede
convulsing on its unit of grey

"I got this reason, irrelevant, translation
I can't get used to the flow or the system
convulsing on its unit of grey…"

Brush Stroke Blues

When it's time for you
and your brush stroke blues
paint your house inside
so you can always hide
from the voice you hear
through a painter's years

Under moss and grass
ornamental glass
caught the sun and glanced
and the light was chance
and the brush stroke fled
Picasso blue and Rothko red

You can always feel
when that brush stroke's real
when that bristle splits
skin and bone and artist's wit
the turpentine
bleach the love
and beat the canvas

SLEEPING PARTNER

Maria Imbrium

I'm drifting home without you
pulling my hair without you
craning my neck to find you
still drifting too far without you
like leaves in a whirlpool
reverse image branches
my arms: blinding frostbite
and the never known agreements
short fuses and the wires
as you spy upon the moon
Maria imbrium
undress between the raindrops
a flood upon an ocean'
you dig around for scarlet
in a ragged sandy trail
still too bright between the branches
I can cover you with a shadow
you undress between the raindrops
still scared of being scarce
and I drift from home without you
crane my neck to find you
bullet hole within a black hole
and the leaves within a whirlpool…

Instead of kissing
you believe your god of wishes
your throat believes it's open
and you're the moon upon the ocean
with its guarded Latin secrets
still too removed to be with it

Maria nectaris
magnet sea upon the sweetness
can't hear the planet sing

I waste the time away
taking notes through telescopes
loving you through sun view
my burning solar flower
I waste the time away
burning garden blackness
back into my night
it's not like we are resolved
but I feel it getting stronger
I love the planet view
I love what planets bring
I love the planet sing
La la la
ah, Maria, it's you!
With your moonflower blues
old Manhattan direction
like the last pages
of the reflection
noir fiction at its dead lover best
I soaked up your story
then I buried it on the moon

Obsession Stares Back

Obsession stares back
says if you were my sister
you'd be my lover
obsession stares back
says you'll be my brother
as well as a lover
across rooms threading your mind

past the people positioned
the dark wear and shadow showers
obsession leaves a line
like Theseus did
shrinking cracks to the chambers
the memory palace
it's all we have
obsession in chambers
most of the doors closed
most of the sound stifled
most of the light replaced with instruction
madame estuary
monsieur le tight line
the rite time
wound up so tight
you can see your reflection
the reflection is down
the double meaning expelled on the moving mirror
so be my sister
so be my lover
talk like Jack and Julie
play like Jack and Julie
in our cement garden
obsession stares back
and kills the frost on the window again
left for hours to talk into the blackness
no glimpse of light on the captive floor
as the obsession stares back
sweet talk back
words encrypted on festival walls
read through filters and wet frames
and back to our chambers
just like Jack and Julie
obsession stares back
we're not decadent

we just drink from the same glass
we're not lovers
we're just siblings who dream!
we sing our cryptic narrative
and lie to the ones we sing to
we're not lovers
we're just Jack and Julie's shadow
shudder to think we shared a womb
madame estuary
monsieur le tight rope walker
don't let the rope slacken
don't fall in your cement garden
where obsession stares back
oh honey, and it stares so hard
that death stare gives life
to every wave your estuary
he's downstairs breathing her in again!
He's downstairs breathing her in again!
He's downstairs breathing her in again!

Picassa

Turn the pages of the illustrations
pencil grey persuasion
the woman is an etching
shine lines indent to the next one

Fake fog betrays a coast
sign language lightning
we see clearer straight hands
aligned against the 'v' of gulls wings

The strange mating of hermetic divide
slick, divine, waist confined
the uneasy trace brushing of pollen painted skin

lust dream spills blot on cartridge paper

My ink drips flickering from the point of origin
she stretches in an 'x' to her points of origin
the enigma points to water mark, water colour
jade pages fade greener in the sorrow light

The Belonging

With the crystal no longer in place
frigid vapour invading a room
condensation from gasping-to cumulus
dissipate vapour
dissipate sounds
relentlessly bound towards heat
the belonging must wrestle
the gull 'v' again
trapped wingless fingers again
motion towards
the sightless uphill approach
approaching the vapour
skin ripples reciting
the nipples like cairns on winter hills

The belonging is moving
the belonging to each other
each other to belong
this might be the darkest
but the sight is enclosed
while fingers unrested
and the motion of toes

If it's down to belonging
then it fits like a glove
bring back to extremities

as they grow back to be alive
the bees are bewildered
as the honey sneaks back to the hive

With the beams and the crosshairs displaced
the belonging snakes stealth
through winter land place
core breathing abstained
as the floor slips away
the shimmer-sounds, sleek in the ear
surrounding the head
as the limbs spring to life
that love is incredulous
it's strapped blue icon
you belong to the stars
but you can't navigate the room
vision dictated
by the dead space of air
the cumulus burrowing
'in the back of your throat
dreaming beyond
the sightless uphill approach
try to expand
I'm sure you can do it
without hands
we belong to those stars
we belong to this room
as the limbs spring to life
they've never been so still

The Black Hive

We lie down, live our lives in the black hive
just extremes, no more memory
no more view from here

a sticky sensation
where we once trusted our wings
I'll slide down you
when you live inside the black hive
you won't fly away
you're safe within the black hive

An afternoon of no shadow
just another kind of mortal
strange as it may seem
I don't wish to penetrate the black hive
whispering, it's whispering
like bees in blindfolds
the black hive shines
in the heat of retreat
afternoon of no sweltering shadow
you don't need to lock the doors
but you will
you don't need to pull the blinds down
but you do
whispering shadow
narcissist shadow
sibling shadow
the nectar infects you
the nectar infests you
and poisons you both
9199
9199
you'll never agree to the sunlight
as you return to the black hive
the comb is ecstatic
you return to the black hive
you'll never agree to the sunlight
but you don't have a choice
like bees in blindfolds

sunk in the black hive

And I'll never let you go
these seasons in the black hive
and you won't walk away
mine until you're not mine
loving seasons in the black hive
the maze in the comb
delivered nightly
the sweetness in the comb
night all day
silk ribbons in the black hive
whisper nightly
delivered
breathing in the black hive
it's made for us to live there

The Sun is a Maze

The sun is a maze
its light from your chambers
folds in on its shadows
in presence of danger
sun is in debt to its labyrinth god
and we're in that maze
coaxed by fixation
silk ribbons ripped long
from tethered obsession
while the sun is a maze
we are cold on the surface
what we do to keep warm
wrapped hard in reflection
the sun showering nectar
on your equine neck
spread length on a secret

those coveted hands
that coveted gown
how we hide from the cold
the sun is a maze
the heat never stays

And now in that maze
a dark generates us
warm in our winter
we wander in place
just to slide off our garments
and slide away morals
the sun points a finger
it's lightning curse stings us
and follows us home
it floods our resources
connecting our limbs
repeating our memories
translating our language
pruning our roses
igniting our bodies
mixing our drinks
persuading our cravings
threading our deserts

Young Magician

Fluid stalagmite
I can make you disappear
to breathe over long
remembering in your air
they tried to throw me off the scent
but I threw them off your scent
remembering in your air
fluid stalactite

hang toe to toe
a flourish of hands
the hey presto moment of reveal
nocturnal nectar
neck to toe
and again
I can make you disappear
seal up the wound
like I seal up the tomb
a soft twilit journey in pharaoh stars
poles and the cross hair
fluid letter h dominates the room
swing low
hey presto
jets magnified by black lenses
scalding escape
and other eureka moments
to hold and watch that alchemy
the hushed whispers
the hustled alchemy
promise to nectar
red horizon across the black lens
fluid letter h
in the kingdom of cross hairs
and you disappear
in a cloud of blue ether
light as a feather
thin as the poles that hold you
pull to magnetic north
pull to magnetic south
swing low
until I go
open sesame
swing low
until I go

open sesame

L.W.W.

Revealing.
Lie down
horizon strained against the myths on sea
sous le lit
dans le placard, dans le garde-robe
un couer
un couer de lion
the lion, the witch and the whisper
dissolving in the same hole
it's raining sleep
dans le garde-robe
couche couche.

Private Screening

I wish I was at your private screening
more than you'll ever know
curtains each side of a halo
to feel the precise line of shelter
on train tracks
through shimmering fields
I wish I was at
I wish I was there
the dark wooden floor
the frame not detached
but an aerial view

VARIOUS

Jubbergait Nurse

Nurse, you're all I have left
these souvenir bath chair excursions
photo box pictures for Mandy and Richard
proportionate eyes
mixed with sunken eye paradise

Nurse, the forecast today
blurred hieroglyphs snatched from the papers
the cross-eyed disclaimers
can run their own races
me and nurse flutter our fancies away

Saliva Beach

Vinegar waves slowly appear
left to the others digging in sand
worms collect coins divining for joy

The last drake forsakes both of its wings
too old to scarper
the sun's here to bleach all of its bones
saliva beach

Harbour Days II
(study for portrait of Anne Frater)

In these days between vision,
your hand that dissected the ocean,
that force fed an era of answers,
so broken,
slow motion,
those lines between islands,
the orbiting ash,
present gifts on your beaches
of dubious worth,
this here is a gull,
five days dead by submerging,
this might have been glass from a bottle,
now rounded smooth enough to swallow,
a rope wrapped with seaweed,
like the opposite of flags,
alongside comes THE DOGS
hands digging for sandworms,
while they churn up a jawbone
half-grinning, half-mimicking,
for the key to the island,
when the tide is up high,
is the inverse of a pattern
on the beach where it lies.

This is sand just like years
between the wrecks of machine works,
quietly praised and high held
like volcano-torn church bells,
while the sea howls its' psalms,
it will bite back the beaches,
reclaiming its gifts

like a petulant child,
there are walls round this ocean
for privacy's sake,
and they look like the islands,
gnawed through by us gannets!
Sword swallowers in granite!
There is none that will trespass,
as we soak our fiestas,
great minds will meander
like bullies on treadmills,
and we move just like sharks
too exultant for danger,
nothing gets in the way when
the heart is displayed,
nothing gets in the way,
next to harbour days.

I Invented the Mirror

I invented the mirror, maybe out of spite,
its silver sting forgotten after midnight
its creeping magpie shadow,
now a magnet for a temptress,
its shredding truth will leave its subject
disarmed or defenceless

It has a way of keeping weaklings
locked away for life,
its physics and fragility
can turn into a knife

I invented the mirror
maybe for a laugh,
but not for any money
or some gloried epitaph

Reflections borne of sun and bone
describing sunken eyes
and even black interiors
will burn through your disguise

A mirror is hysteria
read backwards palindrome
an icy film between us both
that lives inside our home

I invented the mirror
to undo all deceit
and compensate for debutantes
and icons you won't meet

All glass and faded majesty
on pedestals of lies
will topple in the rising sun
and burn through your disguise

Survivor's Guilt

The pipe length and the length of life
anonymous and uncertain sight
the crawl of mercy to window eyes
the metal anguish, the mercy cries
it never rains if I stay like this
the walk of thunder the worst of bliss
collisionism collective crash
the steam of tears that ignites the past

I walk through suffering
destroying dialogues I built
to clutch and hesitate
the solace of survivor's guilt

To stagger out of the stab wound dry!
Still soaking wet from the cutthroat lies
the clustered ageless, the engine's grace
untested drugs on a wordless face
it never rains because it's pelting stones
the birds dismembered and the engine drones
the fury settles, feeding on itself
survivor's guilt belongs to someone else

SPECIAL PROJECTS

LARGO

Ice soaks you in silence
by the time the vice is broken
heavy creatures,
do they sap us of the whispers?

Goading ice bars light the brace
where afternoons clap backwards
of the shadows
we were old enough to choose

Largo's find is thrashing home again
it's never one to wait until the end

Will not dogs betray their masters?
Far beyond this prayer hour?
Splintered shape suit
don't retrieve us in these climes

Father wastes us bled and stagger
in his anxious skin
throat is riddled
with the sores of afternoon

Largo's find is thrashing home again
it's never one to wait until the end

Sleep bonnie babe
sleep for an age
sleep while we pray for our lives

As friction dropped its method to
the shaking floors that bear you
inflicted smiles that frame you out for good
the starving rooms, the leaded ice
that beats you by its bladed hands
still wanting for its double back in pain

Largo's find is thrashing home again
it's never one to wait until the end

Oh but pilgrims, needy pilgrims
glisten like the stealer's hand
burn their wares
in the places of their birth
father's shirts unworked will waste us
urgent bones to save us
deliver us to the places of their birth

Largo's find is thrashing home again
it's never one to wait until the end

Sleep bonnie babe
sleep for an age
sleep while we pray for our lives.

Pray'r

I wrote a prayer,
I was afraid out there,
the craft of his might
wrote back to me, praise him.

His world drew a gun, and aimed at a measurement,
slowly but surely, by will of his aim,
his bullets made waste the terrain… praise him.

Stab the eye, dimly, and leave it with dignity,
that christ is mine,
robbed of its dignity,
his world to a stony halt,
when his wings burned
in the felon sun,
dreaming that no one but he could fly...
spine, repeats spine, repeats spine,
and sorry it grew this way,
wing delivers wing, delivers wing,
black sand where it burned,
and leaving with praise.

Strayed

A missing knock will leave you strayed
unheard of flight
and the hands go back
to try and make the sound go away
last hands over / sight my arms
seethe with flight

On streets you spend with saintly name
under control of beliefs you stole
a crime can be forgiven by fear
crippled tick tock
in a city built on fleeing disgrace

What will the north bring you next?
All subjects you breathe on
you cannot buy.

Wake 1

I walk sleeping in naked grey gardens,
underneath weeping fruit trees,
torn open
by the dignity of the night,
all disfigured by daylight,

The darkest colours may be soft to touch,
they may disappear,
once given in to decay
in dimensions.
Warped and melting,
saddened and angry
wearing their own tragic lives
in heavy dark gowns.

The Call Girls

In time extreme
fire mazes
lose your other
less shaken signs,
you've carried rods of worth,
forever sliding your loan,
in secret brazen midnight hits the scorn
of unlit wombs,
decades of unreason pass you by
and seek you grown.

As spite bears never wonder past,
your early phases blink to mine,
soliloquies die quicker than they breathe
in flooded words,
forget the lady listened

as she walked back to embittered rooms,
dropping guilt and silver
as she leads you through.

Wake 2

In waking
I realize the moment of absolute emptiness
in waking
I realize that I have been tricked
out of an eternity of rebirth
in waking
I can only howl at myself. Again.
The night grins ironically at its own restrictions,

How can anyone destroy conclusions
and carry solitude on their backs,

For lack of anything better to do.

Wake 3

I must build shelter,
I build from the ashes
of so many widows' suicides
and paint my body
with the blood of the poets.

So help me.

Running asleep
through too many empty nights
the stars do not reward me
but catch me on fire
and I breathe kisses

for those who died in pain.

Y

Is this a Y shaped trophy,
inside a Y shaped mouth?
Meeting dark, loud won,
unreward for the undone.

Hold up your cards, be they low or high,
oh, sand covers jewel,
how the steam soaks the pool,
hold up your cards,
be they pictured or flat
is this a sunburst satire,
inside a sunburst mouth.
Shadows long dug deep,
so deep to reach
dividing time and touch.

Cold in the story of shapes unsaved,
a walking downward to otherhood,
walk in the wane,
walking as one from disdain.

Hold up your cards,
some are defaced,
drop them!
Gone on for too long!
Torn in the game they became,
fists down in fright!
Immobile, the ice stays awake,
ordered, I am innocent night-time
to ache in otherhoods steam.

NEW TOWN NOCTURNES

Reclining Figure

A gambler in training
word risk or worthless
trained by rain.
Soaked heat
of gambler's deceit
roulette wheels
Beckett wrecked
and obsolete
spring and cycle motion
turns to clay
in the middle of the play
courtesy of the writer's
fractured Italian hand
or his poker-faced insolence

Colours on the painting you bet on
fade like the wall it's been set on
loss is yours
and you spin out behind the canvas
grasping at pigments
lashing at ligaments
defining in segments
a race too unrun
from a staggered dream
where you throw down
the view from your roof as collateral
the kitchen sink feel of
dusky autumnal tenements
their pockmarked walls
charred by smoky revolutions

Bird song, bet song
how many and how long?
Future diamonds
airborne after the centre of coal
some domino effect distance
wine into water into glacier
reverse nature, flutter on horses, reverse nature
cocaine friction into
fractured hand
bend those fingers
back to their Cyrillic signals
what admonished, and where?
And what to say when
the perfect frost is interrupted?
What to do when the warm breath melts
your section of the ice?
The startled lamp standards
still illuminate the glaze
where you felt frightened
the non-vitals clustered slowly
in sepia pools of light
a gambler in training
his wands and watchwords
dust in the twitch of an eye
sleight ace
and conjuring
as far as I

And what to say when
lovers are divided by a simple mist?
The paring down of coronations
to a room of monochrome size
flicker wrist
folded wings resist, gambling centres, gambling calms
but nothing placed on corrupted arm

again, spring cycle, motion, clay
voided earth dug river deep gray
rambling song
gambling song

Finally, enough eaten away
to allow a view of the ocean
straight, separate waves
blank as shallow pardons
thin as it's glassy shoals.
What is wavering and mountainous
but your back as viewed from behind, as you
curl forward in prayer, or maybe fatigue?
The strength and solace of your white spine
a refugee from some dismal concerto.

Una

Sandalwood,
collapsed with imagined tide
into the epic black spikes,
a rose in debt
startled by sweat
near the flash photos of her skin,
the scarf is present
the earrings present
the curling lights
through the tunnel
on King's Stables Roadthe curling stalactite breeze,
as we stare at traffic from above the trees,
a rose in debt
a rose reflect
within the blossomed crosshairs
a middle meadow march
morning whirlwinds in the name of art

a more rhythmic Modigliani
sandalwood:
scent of silent space
up another canyon of a staircase
from the windows faded vistas
stratosphere harps
sound to wisdom
in the way only the Scots know
and then we were stuck fast to our minutes,
the lines buzzing tidy swarms
as we disappear time,
you cannot breach this silence with anything
Una, yours for the taking
your sound of Holy Corner
your verses getting warmer
your fictions on bonfire night
your boudoir in its orange light
maybe sometime later
we will walk and talk in rhyme
you'll bring up your pages
and I'll try not to kiss you
remember such walks?
Remember how sighted?
And I only imagined your house
and its absence of parents,
its conduit to opium, strange paintings and wine,
and I only imagined YOUR poems
with their bickering rhymes and radiance
but here between your words is an absence
the voided vistas
travelling bullets to the city outside
the muted walk past ruddy strangers
it took a turn
three of us sharing one coat on the soaking walk home
"Una, can I crash at yours?"

Sandalwood.
Epic strikes of the light on its leaves
curious pearls
plunder forth from heaving distance
you mimed:
"Tomorrow, 1, at the Scott's Monument, we'll talk more there"
and I stood on the heart of Midlothian
spitting
all by myself
Una: your fictions take route in imagined decades
spikes of time
withered by a brass begging bowl
the detailed but meandering script
a band around the lip
ring above the muted soil and a dying aspidistra
sandalwood again
this time its traces
brush against your legs
as we turn the Dean Cemetery into a maze
the four, no, the five of us
our own music by the heavy slapping
of trees in the dark
why close your eyes to blink
when sweet darkness drowns you?
Why even speak if your words are
carved in the stones in front of you?

The nearness contingent
your hands define
the braille of the soil
of a freshly dug grave
looking back now at these scratched over exposed photographs
it appears so brazenly erotic
you, how your eyes shut when you smiled
us, retracing our steps

through shadow's triumph
layers of hastily drawn maps to distant parties
spill out of your pocket
half a phone number?
Half an address?
Or try throwing stuff at the window
until someone opens the door.
Or we can stay here.
Sandalwood
sandstone
true granite in the Grassmarket
everything is a walk home at night
everything
but we can never remember where we were
layers of maps
smudged ink from your cartridge pen
mad sister
elusive brother
islands
oddly shaped
fertile or barren
in the Firth of Forth
a reflection in reverse
of some clandestine constellation
lips blown out of the water
city view at night from the Firth of Forth
ancient minds peel back the layers of the city
Una! Look!
The stretched-out churches and buildings
under the bell sounds: Faure, the requiem
Una. Listen.

Lovers on St. Stephens

To take a tiny corner of it
just when I am dreaming
knowing that my heart cannot be there
and knowing that your heart
is pretending to have forgotten.

But these Georgian ceilings heard us
and through skeletal cracks they watched us
and through the gaping windows
the rushes of equestrian air felt us
but we were left alone to our painting
lovers on Saint Stephen'sgarden over garden
and your body over rain
we crawl back
from the cramps of our friction,
the sting of our detail.

The New Town streets my charcoal drawing
and there are you in grainy relief:
umbrella obscuring
these insatiable eyes
the New Town streets a backbone
to my meandering verse,
your fragile massage
on serpentine spine
as we spring for the blackouts
to further move the morning.

The New Town streets with this spiralling sound
steps and laughter,
hurried stairwell
promised wine and cigarettes
for a long afternoon.

Lovers on Saint Stephen's
as we thought we saw Nico
her shadow and story
eclipsing the water
and we hold our breaths
but it might not have been her—her shadow blending into the
    close door.
a match struck on the cover of your diary,
its bluish plume disappearing
into the antiquary throng.
"I have a plan to paint you while you're running"
you whisper
"running naked down the water of Leith, drunk, in the wee hours"
"let's smoke this joint and I'll get my paints out"
…and we were lovers on Saint Stephen's,
with its bells, and its book-lined everything,
a languid river
of vino verde and Yeats
doubling over itself
from here to Cannonmills.

And we left the flow to resin our bows
the climbing lights of East London Street
propel us to steal another's roses,
silent is the world now
save for the flickering cough
from up or across.
To take a tiny corner of it
just back to my own waking
if only you'd pretend with me,
lover in the New Town
frail against iron rails,
playing roughly with your sketch padsmoking and drawing.

These strange dappling patches

of time faded green
reflected up upon our necks
from the season swelled river
this grassy sinew escaping our grips,
as we roll into these urban valleys
lust almost hidden behind a tiny mews house,
the frigid morning air claps its hands
on your slight but off-white thigh
a strange version of piano, cloudy,
ragged, out of a tiny radio
trying to make sense of its own wretched skyline.

Bon vivants on Saint Stephen's:
joints and stolen port on the roof
Satie from a well-worn cassette
and I almost woke up.
Enough to know you wouldn't pretend like me
but enough unknown
that your hallowed worth
is still ambling towards me,
cigarette
donkey jacket
shoulder bag of pencils and paper
under decidedly amber sky.

Then whiter than halo streetlights
cutting piecemeal
between moon and nocturne
turning our paintings to lazy monochrome
and our books to unreadable
but we felt it, no?
Attic rooms, basement hideaways
windows like theatres, curtained and blazing
smoke replacing applause
chimneys like plot thickened clusters

a life between the echoes of horseshoes,
this city is a pendulum
and we are the fulcrum
washed slowly by its vivid arc.

The whiter than halo streetlights,
colliding majesty with the occasional headlight
and we are still on Saint Stephen's
shallow breaths do the trick,
arms stretched from the icy coronas of your shoulders
to the fingered dusk of your thighs,
and I feel like I am lying
because we are so worlds apart,
but a bond so close
that not even telepathy
can decode it
and we dreamed the same dream,
and you left your match scratched notebook
in there for me
on top of a ladder of all places,
in a room where you were painting,
trying to get the detail of the cornice just right,
your hair was shorter and you wore a dress,
and I couldn't reach the book
outside
tons of different versions of us walked by:
some laughing
some drunk and arguing
some were even singing
all young.

All lovers on Saint Stephen's.

The Horse and Thrown Rider

And there we hid waiting for trains
our souls shaken, unbalanced
between aqueduct and viaduct
our crosshairs
on the runaway horses
buried beneath
the shrapnel of ashtrays and leeches
the graffiti with its backdrop of rust and cancer
itself a species endangered
a word play
almost galvanized by fiction gangs.

Look to you, Union Canal blue
in this pastoral danger night
where the bodies float aimless
between regiments of swans,
where factory ushers in night barges of ruin
empty but for coal dust
lying diamonds in the moon
Union Canal blood
flows with no tide,
an amputee of the city
splashing dank
up the back walls of hulking tenements
lifeless scar
for the runaway horses
galloping, sounding like muted applause and distant
for the thrown riders
themselves twisted on the path
Union Canal blind
too dark for even its mysteries.

Union Canal butcher

match tae a leech
underground thunder
on body dumping public darkness
this is no stranger to night stalking
swan, head under wing
black between biting frenzy
and how many darknesses to come
one implodes within another
mental tribes of glue sniffers
carbuncular with ruby glaze
an open flame
match tae a leech
the flame igniting the blood you lost
and you're trying to syphon it back into your veins
it does not matter how many birds there are
they will always just be these flightless lumps
on this syrupy swamp of water
one outfights the other
and the air starves the metal out of the bridge we are crossing
beaks snapping at our skinny ankles
wings slapping at out frantic eyes
our wishes trapped like flies in amber
beneath the weight of our fear
dragging blind fingers through tideless water
waiting for it to belch its blackness
back across the aqueduct
just like our own dark towpath
a walking nocturne to murky futures.

And all the lights went down on Meggetland, Saughton and
    beyond
hiding a curious crime scene.
The playing field
a blood-soaked page of prayer
now being defaced

the cold prized my heart from its shell
dragging metres into miles
deeper into down
midnight, like spilled ink over my days
midnight in fountain bridge
the lifeline on my hand
superimposed over an aerial view of the Union Canal
as it tries to strike
your shaded assignment
match tae a leech
Union Canal kill
match tae a leech
Union Canal fill me with your blood water
okay, I'll admit it
I'm feart, I'm FEART
the horse and thrown rider
dinnae grass me
riding helmet bob bob bobbing
heed throb throb throbbing
and there we hid waiting for trains
in the ditch, by the tracks
seeing how close we could be
to the trains
to the trains.

Causewayside

Causewayside is waiting there
it might as well be winter
suffer sirens, rakish, everywhere
the mist boils over into cold
how many hearts
how many pieces
buried stranger in the wrong way,
on here we bidetaking our silence from Causewayside

Let's take a gander
at the place where the pathless
cross the most and Iwill try not to reflect them off me

And after I thought love was free
and it was scattered wild
like beasts hair on barbs
blown like stubborn clouds
by wind from the shrouded headlands
"it would be good to be lost"
I thought as the white spirit
spilled behind the gorse
"it would mean it wouldn't matter"
I thought as the last match didn't light my roll up

Causewayside, seen from above
such stems of beauty recoiled
back from shifts found under silence
"je suis desole" as I try to revive you inside my coat
it's just the thought of Causewayside at 2 AM
just a feeling or an omen
like the tang of the sub-zero in the air
whisky and panic
cigarettes, remorse
we laughed as we scaled the graveyard wall

Me and you, sentient in our special layers of night
only WE could live here

The roots of life reflected down in
your spectacular eyes
just a memory, but THAT memory

Like fucking on smack when you feel like you'll never come
sword swallower running blind through a metal detector

this is paradise, danger and disappointment
meeting in the same place
the clouds like ghosts of breasts
hanging over the Firth of Forth

Truth spirals like gulls in the cold
Causewayside, too raw to cry
no gatherers of tales or yarns
no back talk or whispers under breath
just clenched on glass
to make things feelvision clouded by moving fiercely
surrounded by some ancient volcanic ash
I can't keep plundering the same memory
even if it is the only memory.

Cairn

And what if I end up on this sightless journey?
To again, after this dense clay brick of time
leaving the 5 AM silence of Holy Corner
for that elusive bronze age cairn.

To walk with that shoddy gait,
stammering and peeling
my air wretched with Players No. 6,
mixed with slow burning Holy Corner leaves,
the smoke denies the clarity
as I walk on regardless,
my sky held aloft by mere steeples,
from here to Hillend,
I'm downhill and deepened.

What charges the blackened sides
of life as I walk in that sort?
The change dust blows

in its own majesties,
whipping and skirling against the wa',
the moss wars "by the banks near the station,
the slow blend of street
into the grand ascent of hills,
and here begins the distillation of yearning and passion:
the collected losses
like the slick hard pebbles
in the reservoir,
the curious grey of its pall,
the furrowed ripples of its meditation.

Here I find myself in the city's attic,
mulling over its stowed away treasures
it's hillside air,
I climb clasping hands
with its lost lover's language,
again, searching for that cairn.
I never knew you Stanley,
but I knew your words,
and I loved your children,
and I often dreamed of
walking over Bavelaw with you.
And right now the journey's vehicle
is running on the scant fuel
of memories and fiction,
brought on by my shameful decades of distance,
I wish I could be home!
And I wish it wasn't now!
An aching heart makes it rain black bullets,
so cold, and straight through ye,

The silence of Holy Corner,
shattered by its bells

And I woke up on Bavelaw
at once predator of rain
rabbit footholes dot
the silent war landscape.

Bavelaw to Holy Corner
a circled route
getting lost in its own fragments
and I push against Saint Peter
and I walk from a first communion
with a dead father
distorted maze of prayers and fear,
wind will always be sharper than me
rain will always be colder than me,
limbs tumble and collide
crossed out version of the Pentlands,
and why could I not walk with you and you and you?
Maybe cut to shreds in the gorse.
Stanley, I don't know if you felt the nettles on your ankles
you maybe did,
I don't know if you heard the land mine rumours,
you probably did.

And god, how I love your poetry,
and god, how it pushed my heart all these years,
and I don't know if you
saw those gray bottles washed ashore
from the still gray of the reservoir,
but I'll wager you did.
YOU are my Bavelaw,
steeples bending under a mass of sky,
whispering stretched under a mass of sky,
yes, I was there all winter, too.
steeples snap like needles
puncturing the Pentland sky

poems in crisis leak gushing from the ruptured rapture.
I should have tried harder to find you,
shorn grass makes for a glib path,
I should have tried harder to find you,
maybe with binoculars from a ward in the P.M.R.

Maybe you knew of me
maybe Alison mentioned me in passing
or maybe I walked near you
on a day just like today
collars turned up and caps pulled down,
noses streaming,
arms hugging thin coats around us.

I carry a sorrow
as big as the reservoir,
as wrinkled as its clammy metallic surface
on this treacherous day,
feet soaked in the burn
hungry
but the darkness that pilfered gem of saluted beauty,
it's nights like this, boy.

And I fell asleep on Bavelaw
dreaming of the predator rain,
clawing my way through the roots and soil,
spitting lichens from my lips,
flame stained and half remembered,
drinking the predator rain,
flayed by thorns.
And collapsing on to nests of the flightless,
my world of you,
you may have found that cairn,
I fell into a new kind of absolution at Bavelaw while at my rest.
Maybe this is what you meant, because in your poem, you gave up,

that pilfered darkness of undiluted beauty,
a gem at the end of light,
this ghastly ascent,
like a ladder up black hill,
rung by rung to night electric,
you can almost hear a music,
a churchy whisper.
I am asking if I can carry a wee bit of what you had, Stanley
just climb up this ladder to nothing.

Bavelaw in minus time:
its soily essence coating my veins,
its magic staining layers,
frostbite on ancient twigs,
and I try to shape words out of the sticks to leave
for you a message on Bavelaw,
so that you have it in time.
I never knew you, Stanley,
but I love your words
and I love your children
and I will walk Bavelaw with you.

BANDS

ACID HORSE

No Name, No Slogan

Unquestioning, undaunting
the silence of language,
anonymous hands,
with a nameless device:

No Name!
No Slogan!

It's safe to say
the attention span is intact
undivided;
anonymous eyes outside
shall remain
unenlightened,
information regurgitated
and forced into machines:

No Name!
No Slogan!

Attention cycle never broken:

No Name!
No Slogan!

Here, the edge is thin,
and skin is far too thin,
so thin the device divides
and cuts up time
and again…

No Name!
No Slogan!

MINISTRY

Never Believe

Is everybody in?
Is everybody in??
The shit action is about to begin…

I made my servants light fire to the city
hysterical laughter at the last of the decorated jewels
I remained drunk for the whole damned war
I owe nothing, you cynics do all the work
I let go of my hand to save this idiot bastard
bastards!

Me and my cellmates have lost the game forever
the sun shines and I freeze my balls off
I want so much to remove your mask
and deliver your now rotting flesh from evil…

Circumstances!
Circumstances!
Circumstances!
Circumstances!

But I'm only allowed to touch what I know
and all that I know are hypocrites
liars and witches
who burned in the name of lucidity

You'll never believe
never believe
never believe
never believe

We haven't much time left...
"Evening will come
and with its equivalence,
no tethered animal would fear to coax,
they ask of us favours we cannot fulfil
they ask after us and we smile..."

"Course and condition a trial for fenceless fields
we'll go further, we'll go for the green,
as sickly a salvation for future fears..."

You'll never believe
never believe
never believe...

Cannibal Song

Dehumanized
lobotomized
thrown into a cell
swallow your pride
in an infant mind

Thrown into a cell
a punishment fit
for a crippled mind
don't do that to me
criminals, subordinates, all laughing at me

Life is hell
forever fighting
a deficit mind
we're all left alone and poisoned
a sickening crack
a sight worth seeing

Dehumanized
lobotomized
thrown into a cell
swallow your pride
in an infant mind

Don't do that to me
don't do that to me
force breaks our back
time preserves, fearfully

You know what I said
hideous in strength
thrown into a cell
a punishment fit
for a crippled mind

So What

Scum-sucking debilitate debauched
anal fuck-fest, thrill Olympics
savage scars supply and sanctify
so what? So what?
So what? So what?

You said it!
Sedatives supplied become laxatives
my eyes shit out lies
I only kill to know I'm alive
so what? So what?
So what? So what?

So what, it's your own problem to learn to live with
destroy us, or make us slaves

we don't care, it's not our fault that we were born too late
a screaming headache on the brow of the state
killing time is appropriate
to make a mess and fuck all the rest, we say, we say
so what? So what?
So what? So what?

Now that I know what is right
I'll kill them all if I like
I'm a time bomb inside
no one listened to reason,
it's too late and I'm ready to fight
so what? Now I'm ready to fight!
I'm ready to fight!
Fight!
So what?

TV Song

Tell me something I don't know,
sell me something I can't use,
push the buttons,
connect the goddam dots.

Live in thief in my bedroom, bathroom
commodity, sodomy,
glass arch enemy,
promise everything,
take it all away,
give it a rest,

You're lying through your teeth,
you're lying through your teeth.

Who, what, where, why,

who, when did you say the earth would stop turning,
when did you say we all would start burning?
When should I make a pledge,
should I listen to the voices in my head?

Connect the goddam dots!
Connect the goddam dots!

Who am I trying to impress?
Who could care less?

PIGFACE

Electric Knives Club

I'm stranded,
may the sin rush through my rigid hands
the list of staggered treasons that define the gang
the edge does not a bloodbath make
you plug it in, you plug it in again

I'm sanguine
but you're looking drained and spent.
the thing about the knife club is
the discontent
and the membership dismembers you
"Do you wanna be in my gang?"
"Do you?"
You join the club, you join the club again

Electric knives
electric rite of passage
hire a cleanup crew
there's nothing further you can do
don't panic, lift the phone and call

Example
of a flight risk on a wingless roof
between the law and 40 stories of blood we drew
do you want to jump or don't you?
You throw yourself
you throw yourself again

I've landed
but my mantle shifted sides today

electric knives "decide the side without me" day
all the floodlight blood ignites you
go up in flames
go up in flames again

Electric knives
electric rite of passage
hire a cleanup crew
there's nothing further you can do
don't panic, lift the phone and call
the blood has left exotic patterns on the floor and wall

I Can Do No Wrong

Take a look outside
because I'm walking on glass,
thin ice in the future—
or a voice from the past,
forsaken dreams decaying
in the fourway zone,
you better look outside,
because I'm coming alone,

How many nights before I sang an innocent song?
Rejoicing in my ignorance,
I could do no wrong,
I took a look outside
for the first time afraid,
outside the glass was shattered,
where one time we laid.

I could do no wrong.

So I drowned my emptiness
between lie after lie,

poured myself another,
and then started to cry,
"Shame on you for weakness!
go back where you belong!"
Poured myself another,
I could do no wrong,

I could do no wrong.

Little Sisters

Cowardice muscles turn to torture
the waking time is low
in between the cut from top to bottom
nerve ends grow
how many days spent screaming blank faced
at the real disease?
Bone collapsing, red eye refuse,
faults within the freeze

They grow, I know
anxious crack the dawn in circles in the flow

The dead appeared in seconds
only slipping murder wept
sweeping under glass decisions
where the only light weights left

How many little sisters breathe
in force fed unity?
Genetic arms unfold the craving night for lunacy

They grow, I know
anxious crack the dawn in circles in the flow

Extend where skin is slated closer to home
instead we celebrated slavery for sake
uncoils the run of runouts
levity and hate

Miss Sway Action

Mood swings and sighs
leaving sand upon the star sign
lost trampled eyes
breathing handmarks on your favourite side

The lost side
emergent airs
we are frostbite
the ladies laughed and swayed
the poison arrow dance hall
beneath us laughed and swayed
all tackles hell and cancels
beneath us laughed and swayed

In the breathing night
the cities almost pray
dance for me
and I'll never go away
free flight and injured motion
carves a ghost
this represented
I won't ever let you go
I won't walk alone
the stair flights to perfection
(one) don't know my name
(two) never breathe the same
(three) all those greedy eyes
(four) never breathe the same outside

(one) don't know your name
(two) but "you'll never walk alone"
(three) pass the blood runs by
(four) never breathe the same
breathe the same outside

(Don't know my name
never be the same again
never know my name
never be the same again)

(One) don't know your name
(two) never feel the same again
(three) miss swayin' action
(four) never dance the same

Point Blank

You always outride
the same outside,
and be diffused
by every
cut-down hide—

You'll be beside yourself
and criminal elements
dig the underground
that stalemate
divides up the same outside.

Foregone the frenzy now,
it seems the edge is torn and cracked,
licking,
cutting,
freezing,

for the longest time
In short the air will be in three,
and warp the floor that holds the heat up
in between us both.

Sent up in separates,
the flame that used to fall between us,
is the deficit,
make mine the sinking sign,
indifferent elsewhere
hangs its heart of heads
above us on the edge.

Weightless

You can't sleep for vagueries or lies,
the silence burns you;
you can't close your eyes,
waiting to be over, to be over.

You can't beat the bigot man
the succour of his slaves,
to be over, to be over,
the pain again.

I'll make it yours,
the first/last
it's hollow logic blind in a stranger,
to be over,
to be over,
to be over.
The first time I saw you here,
your skin was still intact
the sharp arrests you,
your violent face,

in cruciform mosaics.

Sent down for seconds now
the shaking hooks revolve
undecided, undecided
injured out of faith.

Still broken intact
it's pulled apart—blameless prey,
still crying to the years
if sentiment is weightless
too much time is weightless
too much time is weightless.

Still crying to the years,
a stillborn suffers
strangers laugh out loud,
for praise in a predator,
shadows gunned to the wall,
in silence,
bleeding-me-useless,
and shaking the sweat,
to the infants
undermined.

MURDER INC.

Gambit

Wake up—black side of night,
just in time for sacrifice,
bent double in my hand,
face to face with another man.
Who am I to judge you?
I just want to get through to you,
overstepping the margin,
just another diversion.

In the mirror I can see,
coming up behind me,
threats we buried weeks ago,
how was I to know?

Ain't that the truth though—
I'm loud enough to drown you out,
you try to act like a hero,
and come across in your own self doubt…

You seem to think that I'm shameless,
apparent in your rage and hate,
I didn't walk away blameless,
inconsequential, tragic and late.

It couldn't wait forever
the murder of trust,
I'll live with it forever,
as it rots in the dust.

Looks like the gambit is here,

the torrential terminus,
and everything that I knew I'd fear,
stuck between the two of us.

I see us both from the outside,
we walk in circles, unresolved,
I'll take a hammer to midnight,
until this feeling's dissolved...

Looks like the gambit is here...

Hole in the Wall

A light changed hands four times in three,
unwoven, to return in chance, in heresy,
come inside, display and hide
your fair-weather force,
denied and paralyzed between the both.

What's inside?
What to decide?
It's a hole in the wall!
To the world outside.

You don't know anyone,
you don't know anyone at all.

Unexposed to antidotes,
and then covered up,
goodbye demanding friend,
I wish you luck.

Last of the Urgents

Time becomes the victim,
time between the lines,
we display the symptoms,
we display the signs,
what we thought was urgent,
hits us in the face,
what was once important
now becomes debased.

This time...

Disconnect the mainline,
cripple us with nerves,
twist around the war crimes,
get what we deserve
close to what we came for—farther from the truth,
something else to die for,
staring up at you.

This time...

Darkness turns to desperate,
anger turns to light,
forever to escalate it,
doesn't make it right,
what do you think I'm here for?
Why'd you think I came?
Give it to me
and I'll never ask again.

This time...

Last of the urgents,

last to leave the room,
remind me when I say
tomorrow came too soon,
burned into a breakpoint,
dead above the neck,
hold my breath until,
until I see you next.

This time...

Mania

Across the way, where shadows play,
you took me too, we walk on through,
head over heels, we fall in reels,
my mania, my saviour,

Too late to scrape the ceiling with my eyes,
we walked into a trap we built from lies,
and even though we thought that we could see,
a thousand other people just like me,

Let go my hand, like sinking sand,
leave me at least, to drown in peace,
I see it now, there is no doubt,
my mania, my saviour,
I searched your mind for somewhere new to hide,
and left my empty corner to go outside,
I faked a hundred fleshwounds just for you,
for lack of any better thing to do,

And still the bridge collapsed the space between,
replaced the gap inside with silent screams,
raked across the coal—what are you telling me?
before you disappear

let me see.

Motion Sickness

This is the place where fear burns flesh,
love and disease are under duress,
I made a decision some time ago,
to hide in a place where motion's slow…

There, time won't say,
just walk away,
in midnight's empty reasons,
damaged as the day.

I would not stand before deceit,
encouraged only by this heat,
I hear mistakes call out my name,
they haunt me time and time again.
Collapsing consciousness decides,
returns in fragments thrown outside,
believing right to fear the most,
a shattered life becomes a ghost.

There, time won't say,
just walk away,
in midnight's empty reasons,
damaged as the day.

It would not last a frozen moment,
murder's anti-world pours down
and stains the ground I spit upon.

Take this version of my name,
black with agony and shame.
guilt is ruthless in its course.

Blind and lost, see how they run,
cornered people, they may strike,
thriving fury, lost in fright,
open secrets, break the day,
blame the night where liars stay.

Murder Inc.

More than a feeling
sitting on an instinct
breaking out fast
no time to think
if it's live
is it living in my own mind
forced to the ground when I bring it on down
it's a farce
it's unsurpassed
too young to be political, too old to care
what's next?
to be taken out of context
fooled into sellout
making me shout about lies
about compromise
forced, inhibited, unresolute
don't shoot!
just prostitute
with that in mind
don't waste my time

Make the whole thing mandatory
take the whole thing, cut it in two
make the whole thing mandatory
take the whole thing, cut it in two

Vendetta?

Don't know the meaning of the word
and the word is blind
in the adult mind
make haste!
Take sanctuary!
More than a minute in history
it's mine: frozen in time
with a fake fatalism running out in the middle
it's a crime
it's bottom line
end of an era the beginning of the year of
blackout international!
unconditional
in my attitude
make no mistake: we've come to fuck you over!

Right time for double standards
getting stabbed in the back if you look back
criminal minds, criminals want to find
when our eyes are shut, the right place and time
to rob you blind
don't say a word, 'cos we'll use it against you
and you won't have a thing to defend you
time to rethink! Reactivate!
Locate, subvert and terminate!
Insane, but experts with it,
don't need to prove a point, 'cos we live it
altered state: the mandate
the rules of the game do not apply
just go ahead and lie
to one another
but don't forget
we've come to fuck you over!

Red Black

Turning red to black,
alchemical and mania,
you can't look back,
an outside view,
to the constant craze—collapsing and inferior,
the rain came down,
it's burning you.

This is nothing short of power play,
invitation to waste,
in the dawn of a dog day,
rationale defaced.

In the strength of crime,
a cure would seem impossible,
too hard to find—
we all fall down
in a stagnant state
tomorrow could be terminal
this book is closed
they lied to you…

This is nothing short of power play,
invitation to waste,
in the dawn of a dog day,
rationale defaced.

All the madmen came,
and gave us all security,
they stole it back,
and laughed out loud,
at the way we crawled,
from grace into insanity,

the saints marched in,
on top of you.

This is nothing short of power play,
invitation to waste,
in the dawn of a dog day,
rationale defaced.

Supergrass

Your song came on again,
why can't I hear it?
Reminds me of your stormy weather,

At heart you are afraid,
to tell me your secrets,
it's not so much my own endeavour…

Remind me to awake
with your fascination,
I wanna spend some time in you,

To overcome today,
my terror of breathing
I'm breathing in because of you…

I once caught you stealing,
so long ago,
things that I bought you,
how did you know?

The sun burnt my skin,
the moon kept on shinin'
the treasures of my open book…

The pages were blank,
or stained with my whiskey,
I can't believe you tried to look…

But give me some time,
and space just to breathe in,
I swear I'll give it all to you…

I broke down my walls,
and opened some windows,
to open up my eyes for you,

I thought I could believe you
a long time ago
you planted these seeds,
now they won't grow.

Uninvited Guest

Poison dripping gently
back and forth,
between us both,
ascends in increments,
outside where time collides
in sycophantic dead-end lines,
guilt alone will colour truth,
it never needed me or you,
fake confessions burn my night
to waking moments.

Accusations fly like birds of prey,
into the heart of my darkest day.

Climbed the staircase in the rain,
risked my neck for you, again,

if I wanted to I could,
it never does me any good.

What is life without despair?
The elevated moods we share?

Forced to welcome comfort like disease,
take your medicine and leave,
wrap your finger around my past
breaks your skin like broken glass.

Bleed into the paper cup,
drink it down and spit it up,
make a mess upon the floor,
on which you crawl to lock the door.

DAMAGE MANUAL

King Mob

King Mob in a plastic iceberg
smoking water damaged cigarettes
observe as he works your wasteland
pulling punches that you never met
controlled in a listless airstream
jets are breathing in his latex eyes
true to form he is scared to touch them
and your wasteland stays vandalized

Success in a cut glass wardrobe
all the clothes loose like shredded hair
dream escapes to a closet class war
King Mob in a smashed wheelchair
nerve gas for the walking wounded
suffocating in a sadist's prayer
flaming horses on a fading landscape
break the surface but there is no air

King Mob as he vents his anger
throws a brick through the city gates
backfires on his wordless offspring
the population disintegrates
cold steam plus a wash of carbon
drives his mind like an engine room
cogs turning like a flawed stage whisper
King Mob sings a lifeless tune

Surface stop
pressure drop
King Mob

Faded wrists and the risks worth taking
cleans his blade with dreams he froze
metal moments fed on foreign textures
breaks his mind with the things he knows
King Mob at his withered console
electric arcades run on secret oils
flicks a switch and he's the god of anger
pulls a handle and the wasteland spoils.

Age of Urges

Can't move the age of urges
indecent power surges
I can lose my sight
it ain't worth seeing you
reversed in light
you seem to split in two
beneath the age
warped, innocent and left intact
the urge of age
turn/reconcile/take it back
my eyes are cursed and darting
and the shots ring out the same

ring the bell if you're hungry
you've started fighting for less
fill a hole with your money
it's all second best

Break through the force of nature
drape blinds on all your answers
you'll never fall
unless we tell you to
against the wall
you seem to split in two

the word is out
bad liars case an unlit mind
too loud to shout
when you drown aloud in turpentine
force fed-your insults ended
and the words repeat the same.

Top Ten Severed

I am your top ten severed
I am your number one
reduced to fictions dancefloor
and fake delirium
a man of seasoned syndromes
programming mysteries
a man of useless incomes
forgotten litanies

You want some answers quickly,
you write down nothing wrong,
and I inquire discreetly
about your favourite song
it starts all good intentions
it ends in falling hearts
did I forget to mention
it plays before it starts

You cannot play this record
its grooves are dressed to kill
all daylight frames per second
the chances are you will
bring out your dancing party
fill up your little room
your silver eyes enchanted
they glide and shoot the moon

I am your one hit wonder
your Christmas giveaway
I am your stolen thunder
your "no love left today"
a frozen sound diminished
out on the radio
the song is never finished…

Peepshow Ghosts

Baby why d'you wake me?
Is it my idea of eyes?
A thousand sleeping eyes,
it's creeping up to you
like peepshow ghosts they do
a sorry fault of mine
will take you back in time

The peepshow ghosts will fade awayand reappear in you
and if my dead darling stays away
she will break my heart in two

The booths all ragged style
you crawled that extra mile
where the woman ends and shame begins
the world can read your mind
the girl can make you blind
all hostage stolen flesh
will nail you to the rest

I dreamed about the faithless
I asked them passers by
could you wake me if I start to shake
if I should start to cry
remind me of my crime

and every fault of mine

When bitter starts to turn around
and bites your swollen face
the stolen stabbing darkness
the nakedness and starkness
will kill you if you stay
too near to her just pray

Sunset Gun

From the moment I woke
in receipt of a blackmail note
and these curious eyes
a new disease of the last seen eyes

A live christ in the city
I got my black-eyed mind
I'm gonna poison up the wrong way 'round
like a bad design

It's in the way that I'm cold
left dealing with a famished soul
I won't give you the time
it's greed sparked in a goldmine

I can't view your condition
it's as failed as they come
great failures are forced
into our famished eyes with a gun

It's in the way that I'm cold
left dealing with a famished soul
it's all fake as they come
burn my eyes like a sunset gun

Your point of collapse
my mark of indifference
it's all fake as they come
burn my eyes like a sunset gun

It's not like you care
even at my insistence
it's all fake as they come
burn my eyes like a sunset gun

I won't give you the time
it's grief sparked in a goldmine
it's in the way that I'm cold
left dealing with a famished soul
it's all as fake as they come
burn my eyes like a sunset gun
burn my eyes like a sunset gun
(like a sunset gun)
burn my eyes like a sunset gun
(like a sunset gun)
burn my eyes like a sunset gun
(like a sunset gun)
burn my eyes like a sunset gun
(like a sunset gun)

Stateless

You hide high speed out of engine greed
and don't stop to look at the world you bleed
cars carousel on an unmade bed
drive the point home after what you said

Still life in an apocalypse
add some dirt to your endless list
force fed freedom defaced your will

adds an age to the time you kill

This is you—stateless

Stateless
stateless
candidates are waiting
you can't open up
'cos your hands are shaking
waste not want not
images blurred
sugar coated bullet words

Crime spread wide on an ill-timed night
vanishing point after homicide
wait, bear arms out of threat or thrill
don't breathe aloud 'cos they scare you still

Cold conviction for remembered threats
faded flames burn you with no regrets
new exposure to an old disease
breaks the surface with a sense of need

Decaying distance cuts the clock in two
and sends the time back to remember you
graveyard name change, unconditioned spite
resolve recorded in a different light

This is you: stateless inside

Expand

Someone leans against the mirrored marvel
reflecting rascal
anaemic article

the part you least expected
it commands
expand

A flawless life form, the lowest level
rejects the offer you carried further
the talk is all so loaded when you can expand

Expand to reach a surface suffocated
shown equipment too large to break
you lunge yourself to the underground
got to expand

A meagre mission yields amazing purpose
rebuilds your offer and flies it homewards
it's past tense past attentionwhen you land, expand

The perfect host for the endless story
the missing motion, the frozen ghost
the heart stops part achieving
when you stand
expand

Denial

Something more graceful felt like leading you to war
it sounds so distasteful more than what you're fighting for
more flights of stairs derailed, your ascent it falls so slow
your body and your love impaled on the spikes you left below

Grief turned to currency just like Midas touched it black
like rage in its infancy, you're afraid it might turn back
a flag slashed by injured nights in a fist outside your past
waves only eclipsed by fright in its glory at half mast

You can't beat denial, it's the murder of your past
a line drawn hard and broken down
to lie outside your grasp
I fooled you by way of greed but it opened up your eyes
too deep down in your hallowed nerves
but it came as no surprise

Your silent servant dragged abyss across the ground
to wallow sleeplessly on everything you found
afraid lasts a lifetime and it crosses paths with mine
lost fades it's energy, in the end we both but shine

So ends disgraceful, ride me back to where I rain
controlled and quarantined
unpure distressed and stained
your war so makeshift, as if a path through broken seas
your faith so restless as you turn to talk to me

Broadcasting

Fractured signs, they waste my time
they concentrate, they take what's mine
lost they move like fractured ghosts
to empty heads in empty lines

Trapped in frames of empty films
a war is flat in frames they kill
light will char, and edits cut
they broadcast stare, they know they must

Faded raids
before they fold
into themselves
it's done I'm told
acting fast repeats to last

and beats you back
when credits rolled

Build yourself a fame through fire
and douse it out when you require
list your age on lilac page
strength in a crawl
back to the stage

When it's obvious they're not scared of us
they will drag you back to cold
all film burned at source much too fast of course
they will drag you back for more
when your wish runs out they will make you doubt
they will drag you back for more
when your fame runs dry minds will start to fly
they will break before they fold

Broadcasting once
broadcasting twice
broadcasting 1 2 3 4 5

Blame and Demand

We have been worthless
we have been safe
in minds belittled by the threat
of our own ice age

A fall distorts us
and where we've been
rewriting bastards as contenders
sight unseen
in place of angels
butchers hands

too wide to fit through doors of virtue
blame, demand

We count for distance
from human nerves
we count for all the things we take that we don't deserve
all contradictions
will make us stand
to fake the end as the beginning
blame demand

Blame and demand

Damage Addict

Winter bruise, bring home the news
bullet door implore reclaim a crimson fuse
break weight, under gun resolved
sick and solvent blister baby, black absolved

Absolved, stone's throw, hangman, stain

Stone's throw, strangled vice will crawl
steady sordid uniform on hangman's wall
car sick, wheels of bone and stain
misdirected epileptic hangman's game

broken, eternal, nerveless, damage

Work fast, damage addict, clockwork shrine
switch craft, hammer magic war design
clock fast, ticky tocky, undermined
work fast damage addict clockwork shrine

Vice, jagged, crush, vein

Fixed stare, broken unlit life
faded vein eternal cut by unlit knife
drop kick, window crushes arm
stricken hand will nerveless under manual harm

Leave the Ground

Cynical, affordable
lashed down like heaven sent intangible
lucrative, initiative
unbreathing forces stoked on sedatives

Fraternize, romanticize
bring what is spoken for familiarize
overkill, dependable
more human contact will just make you ill
make you ill

That old disciples got a hold of me
I'm sick of walking on the past you see
take your skeletons and run, bye, bye baby
purge your thoughts into the sun
goodbye baby, bye, bye, bye

Leave the ground before us
see how they run
(see how they run)

Scissor Quickstep

All aboard, the ride goes faster
being driven by the spooky bastard
look left, dirt infested
living large with the debt invested

Gung ho, Mr. Murder
could be a while but you look no further
snip, snip, scissor quickstep
cut the line, you are out of your depth

Bring home the bacon bastard
a meaty fringe in a leather casket
fuck that, I eat my offspring
hang myself on a leather heart string

Cut the page from the New York Times
wee, I'm not so bad after all
you'll never get held in my outstretched arms
cause I won't catch you when you fall

Pull the trigger at your picnic table
take the scissors from your baby doll
you'll never get to Heaven with a face like that
and I won't catch you when you fall

Flick, flick, another station
listen hard but I'm losing patience
another aim, absurdest brainwash
another bent pair of scissor outlaws

Sick baby move at a heartbeat
when I'm bloody on a leather bed sheet
blood bitch cancelled reflex
another bent pair of scissor defects

Here baby, I'm out to get you
a broken heart in a broken test tube
a virus scare for those who care
don't look alive 'cause you'll go nowhere

Cut the page from the New York Times
see, I'm not so bad after all
you'll never get held in my outstretched arms
cause I won't catch you when you fall

Pull the trigger at your picnic table
take the scissors from your baby doll
you'll never get to Heaven with a face like that
and I won't catch you when you fall

Revenge Fiction

I'm too close to decide
seems like the page never lied
do you see the fiction at your front door?
this time it's not like before

Just like your shadow in public
your secret floodlights the floor
you got too nervous and left it
and now you're looking for more

Reads just like revenge fiction
some 40s novel re-lived
reads just like revenge fiction
no more excuses to give
no more excuses to give

Don't be confused by my signal
I'm only here to collect
better lifeless than nervous
with nothing left to protect
with nothing left to protect
with nothing left to protect
with nothing left to protect

with nothing left to protect

Reads just like revenge fiction
some 40s novel re-lived
reads just like revenge fiction
no more excuses to give

Reads just like revenge fiction
some 40s novel re-lived
reads just like revenge fiction
no more excuses to give

No more excuses to give
no more excuses to give
no more excuses to give
revenge fiction
no more excuses to give
revenge fiction
no more excuses to give
revenge fiction
no more excuses to give
revenge fiction
no more excuses to give
revenge fiction
no more excuses to give

No Act of Grace

Too much ice on the outside
too much time, to get out
there vacant sways
become angry, nothing faced
nothing followed

It's a vice of disciples

lapse of faith
no act of grace

Moving steals, in as much as we reveal
no encounter, no attachment to
anything less than we corrupt

It's a life but at least
it is contained
no act of grace

It's the fall of a morning
you wake in before
it's the life that is calling
you can't kid yourself

It's the act of you killing
you can't take it back
it's the things that you did
that you still can't remember

The people would rather
you never wake up
there's no act of grace

To the minds, to the greedy
needful kinds
wishing worthless, wishing backwards
wish you weren't here

Stick out loud
stick out gestures
stiff the crowd
no act of grace

It's the fall of a morning
you wake in before
it's the life that is calling
you can't kid yourself

It's the act of you killing
you can't take it back
it's the things that you did
that you still can't remember

The people would rather
you never wake up
or at least you would die for
instead of suffer
there's no act of grace
there's no act of grace
there's no act of grace

I Am War Again

You must have seen me miles away
cannon weight on a steel blade
the night composed of wires alarms
the enemies agrees to make

All my weapons burnt of stamina
abused power behind barriers
all the misdemeanors close their eyes
there is nothing you can do

Dead inside the midnight hits in slow motion
I am war again, I am war again
make the brutal border lines back out of science
I am war again, I am war again

The uniform inside my mouth
spits a cave into the virgin world
glass shattered on the ghost of gods
cuts a path where you can find me still

Carving fuck yourself on floodlit skin
reminds me of the war I'm in
camouflaged and cut devoid of life
the conviction read the same dead

Dead inside the midnight hits in slow motion
I am war again, I am war again
make the brutal border lines back out of science
I am war again, I am war again

Mad Dialect

Take no denial
no for an answer
make a wish and make it total
take a risk and make it fatal
I love to be here
because it means so much to me
I love the action
of a forced conspiracy

The word was strong
but you answered wrong
mad dialects, mad dialects
broken glass of a language
mad dialects, mad dialects

Look for deception
no common truths
link it up to every phone call

say you lied, then hang it up
well, it looks so doubtful
just like everything's erased
the text is backwards
but it is hammered to the page

The word was strong
but you answered wrong
mad dialects, mad dialects
broken glass of a language
mad dialects, mad dialects

Corrupted future
beneath your wires
circuits floored by lie detectors
blackout lights and resurrect
well, I see it surging
just like it burns past other halves
and still submerging
electric future never lasts

The word was strong
but you answered wrong
mad dialects, mad dialects
broken glass of a language
mad dialects, mad dialects

Laugh Track

Area life, concrete mission with a black light
area life, you never listen to the dog's bite
watch what you do, every border is in front of you
watch what you do, area life is going to follow you

Uncontrolling yourself, only seconds to spare

and the hand that you need is the one that's not there
did you walk like a fraud through the slogan you wrote?
And the story you told was only good for a quote

Area life, bunker precinct with a laugh track
area life, cultural etiquette that bites back
do what you're told, weapon traffic without warning
do what you're told execution with a cause

Uncontrolling yourself, only seconds to spare
and the hand that you need is the one that's not there
did you walk like a fraud through the slogan you wrote?
And the story you told was only good for a quote
area life
area life

South Pole Fighters

It's even brittle
they lock hands
to make a line
perhaps dividing
solid forest
saw blades
sightless, flawless
walking sideways
chain could bite
in this white out
scissor teeth
cruelty lip
tireless grasp
frigid spike
glass desert
mesmerize
circulation

South Pole fighters
South Pole fighters
South Pole fighters
South Pole fighters
missing climate
bleeding wind
needle wages
blinking words
ghost of light
no circulation
way of breathing
no more blades
no more walk
no more hide
against a whiteness
black desert
end arena
sightless, flawless
no more breathe
no more shadow
South Pole fighters
South Pole fighters
South Pole fighters
South Pole fighters
it's even brittle
they lock hands
to make a line
perhaps dividing
solid forest
saw blades
sightless, flawless
walking sideways
chain could bite
in this white out
scissor teeth

cruelty lip
tireless grasp
frigid spike
glass desert
mesmerize
circulation
South Pole fighters
South Pole fighters
South Pole fighters
South Pole fighters
missing climate
bleeding wind
needle wages
blinking words
ghost of light
no circulation
way of breathing
no more blades
no more walk
no more hide
against a whiteness
black desert
end arena
sightless, flawless
no more breathe
no more shadow
South Pole fighters
South Pole fighters
South Pole fighters
South Pole fighters
it's even brittle
they lock hands
to make a line
perhaps dividing
solid forest

saw blades
sightless, flawless
walking sideways

Quiet Life

I need to go to the place where the blackouts live
need to roll like a corpse to the graveyard shift
couldn't ask for more cold than a collapsing rock
over consciousness eyes, under electric shock

I need to use these fingers wrapped around this knife
oh, I would kill for a quiet life

Quiet life, oh, I would kill for a quiet life
quiet life, oh, I would kill for a quiet life

Never mind the obsessed, they don't remember
when all of our waking hours were spent submerged again
need a solid year removed from solid light
need to disappear, I need a quiet light

I need to use these fingers wrapped around this knife
oh, I would kill for a quiet life

Quiet life, oh, I would kill for a quiet life
quiet life, oh, I would kill for a quiet life
quiet life, oh, I would kill for a quiet life
quiet life, oh, I would kill for a quiet life

I need to use these fingers wrapped around this knife
oh, I would kill for a quiet life

Quiet life, oh, I would kill for a quiet life
quiet life, oh, I would kill for a quiet life

quiet life, oh, I would kill for a quiet life

Oh, I would kill for a quiet life
oh, I would kill for a quiet life
oh, I would kill for a quiet life

Driven Menace

MENACE
MENACE
MENACE
MENACE

The risk is worth taking it's a shapeless rage
all analysis B-listed on the back page
it's a crime made of mine it's a flawless shrine
it's a message to a man who's lost at his stage

Be careful how you are driven, gets so easy to live
between the gestures of the fingers that you point with
chanting, ha, ha, ha, at your favourite star
like the menace ever liked you to begin with

I'm just a kid whose time expired before the show
unknown menace driven nightly you should know
all the mysteries just irritate and strain
driven menace back again

MENACE
MENACE
MENACE
MENACE

An endless list of surrogates burn agents to the ground
habits formed and commerce broken voices thrown

the menace is mechanical just mediates on speed
medication-given life form never breathe

Most of us manipulate the truth into a loop
repetition then ignition then shoot
madness driven menace as the temper counts to ten
in the shadows from the never know what happened

I'm just a kid whose time expired before the show
unknown menace driven nightly you should know
all the mysteries just irritate and strain
driven menace back again

M E N A C E
M E N A C E
M E N A C E
M E N A C E

I'm just a kid whose time expired before the show
unknown menace driven nightly you should know
all the mysteries just irritate and strain
driven menace back again
I'm just a kid whose time expired before the show
unknown menace driven nightly you should know
all the mysteries just irritate and strain
driven menace back again

M E N A C E
M E N A C E
M E N A C E
M E N A C E

Limited Edition

They follow the forgotten like they promised me so often
moving fingers, charging hymns to other gods
complicated missions, covered convalescing structures
mountains hidden inside more unspoken words

Chimes unearthly bells, before the reason we could never tell
a secret simply liberates the finish
claustrophobic empty and competing to surround you
asking, do you want to hear about the damage?

Do you want to hear about the damage?

EVERYONED

Glass Shall Wake

All afraid the glass shall wake
it's motion scrambles forward
into late but wait
laid flat and scanned nude
fails to allude
too hacked
and too bent out of shape

Curved angels shunt like slowest trains
slow misfires into feathers
to each white and stained
fists braved upon the canvas
heart of wingspan lands
drag your nails against
the ferrous sky

Knife Audition

He's been auditioning knives
only to share in his pride
great the guts of mystery
that perish inside…

Black dark hallways in his time
of his time
auditions expected to start here anytime
on the quiet stage
where the walls are stained
with the opposite of the sunshine
with the opposite of the sunshine

with the opposite of the sunshine

With the opposite of the sunshine
with the opposite of the sunshine
with the opposite of the sunshine

Calls himself the mirror of rage
reflect the back page
drives himself to sunblind fright
it's still dark outside
he's been auditioning knives
only to share in his pride
great the guts of mystery
that perish inside
that perish inside
that perish inside
that perish inside

Friends of Mine

Call it mine
it's all that made me
waiting here alone
too mad, too misty eyed
you're more than afraid here
with all the things you've shown

Used to be's that speed in threes
down on wasted lines sublime
it carries over
it sticks in me like some friends of mine
but I swear the urge was there
just the motion drowned it out

Drown it out

drown it out
drown it out

Failing right before you fall
like you scraped your skin too far
it keels over and stares at me
like the friend you are
and I'm trying to call it mine
just the motion took it back

All of my playthings
playing with me alone
I thought I saw you smile
you more than made me
with all the things you've known

Used to be's… etc.

First to Know

Grievous story ask for my own way back
turning sentence-jewel mode, the answers sat
crime is playing cards for your party
it's never not the illusion of hearts

Hard times/first times
we're the first to know
my side/black light
we're the first to know
we're the first to know

Overshadowed by crisis of a palm less straight
missed the wonder designed by only thrown too late
fear and thunder enthralled by despair
the way back home and there's no one there

Curtains

All the lights standing
built to demand
just to lie upon—
Just below landing
cruelty lasting
—can't retrieve

Red floor to rooftop
my lips just won't stop
it's a sorry plight

Floor to the glass to the rooftop
sometimes I just can't stop
framed like a film in the doorway
wake up
wake up
wake up
look at the film in the doorway
curtains in the screen look up
look up
look up
look up

Dancer's Legs

These pictures swipe at your blindness
sky worth of charcoal
regarded and birdless
breathing lashes some eyeless brine
hung not in order
you are forced to decipher
the way you are godless
begins and ends

The glass in your pockets
the coins from the cluster
the pencil black starved
with its dirt and its curves
This could be a criminal tide
submerged in its own
to throw at your blindness
accuses the namesake
to illustrate chambers
all hung not in order
weapons are wordless
hung so much further

Low End Flight

The waste grew wise
well inside
but it was watertight
I can't describe
careless flame that it would tell a lie
low end flight
then I will meet you by the waterside

Fly so long
fly so low

Lie freezing on an escalator
speech slows down to another sound
what you need when you compensate
for broken cycles
when the break out loud

An issue lost
well straight
to take a second shape

lost sight of ghost
all threats pretend to levitate
low end floats
no crime defines the wasted

Fly so long
fly so low

You Wear It Like Smoke

If you wear it like smoke
no one will know
and no one will effect you
if you roll just like dice
red black and concise
I'm never gonna let you
take the words that you weigh
and scare them away
waiting for a breakthrough
all this cause for descent
you fall then you're spent
I'm never gonna let you

Waste in the water, come inside
wasted blueprints only half the map
trying to swim back in the dark
(If you wear it like smoke
 no one will know…)

If YOU try to choke
no one will hear you
swallow back your birthmark
if you hold back surprise
like blistering eyes
no more angles in the dark

and the face of conceit
it can never be beat
but it can stain you like a cheat
and you roll just like dice
back to heaven and ice
no more swimming in the light

THE HIGH CONFESSIONS

Mistaken for Cops

I'm trying to reach a few decisions
by driving round myself at night
live far enough from running water
and insect shadows in the light
don't want to see no living creature
I'll close my eyes and breathe the smoke
I'll burn the meaning from the pages
deface the language that you wrote

At times the scape is free of danger
connects a focus to a fade
it pulls the mouth from off the mountain
and keeps imposters in the shade
I can't believe a veil is lifting
it just reveals another wall
the bullet holes are soft and drifting
they're closing up just when you call

You try to reach me when I'm stable
and my mistakes reflect a trend
a closely guarded cure of folly
a need, a circumstance, a friend
all thoughts of certainty and purpose
connect like eyeballs in the sun
reveals another wall of injured
the bullets fly back to the gun

I threw the statues on the train tracks
and you mistook them for the cops
headlights are picking out your stone eyes

they just shattered where they dropped
I'm driving round myself at midnight
locked in a car park on my own
I'm trying to imitate the screeches
and mock the silence when I'm done

Along Came the Dogs

Along come the dogs
hide behind the sand dunes on the beaches
not your psychotic armour any more
the dogs stare 'cos they are tired of eating each other
what do you say to no reason?
hiding in the water only makes them angry
try to collect rushes

Along come the dogs
flies on the fruit
lights go out in your passage
a form of wasting away
a form of waiting to come nearer
the wilful digging of soil
the scarring of feet in your sleep
the closed eye uncertainty
move a little / turn a little
along come the dogs
he's reaching into his bag for something
the lights go out
the passage inclined at an angle
the water drifts to the nearest hole
lapped up by dogs
blood clots on the walls
lights get through no cracks
only smoke and distress
the prayers in the hand in the morning

broken voice in the speaker
along come the dogs

The flight wanders
the light stabs
the day cornered
the age race
a cold heaven
a burnt room
a star backwards
a dark noon
you can't hear it
the wall's thick
you drown treason
the knife sticks
the close meeting
the glass flies
the stone rivers
the banks rise
of all cities
of all words
of wires hanging
the dead birds
collapse over
the main thing
and start digging
start collapsing
you start freezing
you lack blood
a street serpent
the last flood
you stole reason
you gave fright
you start freezing
you stab light

Nervous from the neck
part of the charade
how many nights talking?
How many nights talking?
Character you made
how many nights talking?
How many nights talking?

The Listener

I watched as it rounded the corner
the pulse as it slowed to a drone
inverting the parts where it's icy
I waited for something to come

The pictures of war are too cryptic
deliver the message in shards
behind every wall is a listener
behind every tool is a guard

The minutes they try to dissolve us
the minutes they try to decide
the steps that you fall down are slanted
it didn't take effort to fly

The glass all eroding the buildings
it sucks all the life from the street
it scores every wall with graffiti
the journey's as blind as a prayer

The roses are getting corroded
like nothing you'll need 'til the end
the light is all covered by enemies
with nobody left to defend

Dead Tenements

All razors say goodbye at night
the streets are timeless laughter
and all consumed by packs of men
who howl when glass is fractured
you see the close door through the shades
a sea of blood and bone breaks
on top the bottle glass topped wall
will cut your hands to nothing
you're still out on a bender
and I'm trying to remember

All polarized by open doors
dead tenements did surrender
dying waterfalls to blood spills
glass black from revolution
the carriage breaks in crowded steam
the first to fall through station roofs
the first to leave the city
the last to leave the smoke
pull questions from the mystery

War of answers in the end
cascading from the dockside men
all moving ghostly downstream
without a limb between them
coal clustered on the tracks with steam
like the shadows who may steal it
what belches from the stacks to me
but dead tenements again

Chlorine and Crystal

I wanted to breathe
only chlorine and crustal
the windows open up to the waste
and I'm right there
I wanted to fall
I wanted to visit it
I threw my last possession to you
but you're not there

I wanted to stand
pretend I'm not starving
the mirror at the end of a life
like broken hope
I would like to crash
if crashing's an option
but the cycle won't allow it
stay on your feet

The canisters and crystal
they're getting close to me
the metal is dissolving
it's difficult to breathe
if certainty is silence
the chlorine has escaped
the crystal turns to concrete
there is no time to wait

You climbed to the gods
expecting an answer
the windows open to a void
but they are not there
the dialogue closed
and stifled by language

the sting as every bone is destroyed
but you're not there

I Thought It Was Snow, Instead It Was Flies

I thought it was you
I thought it was you
trying to twist your way around in antique blue
the maze at your feet
is trying to deceive you
trying to endear itself to nothing less
I promise you this
I promise you this
move mistakes upon the namesake
until the breathing fades
I promise you this
I promise you this
the cold's already struck the metal
winter catalyst
you're climbing in time
to the hearts on the wall
and fall down excruciating drops
decay the pattern's way
I thought it was snow
instead it was flies
trying to beat their tiny wings
on molten windows
the windows break
little heart shaped beaks
little cuts in wounded wings
and the birdies sing
"do do do do do"

I thought it was here
I thought you were leaving

your concession to the doorway
as you scrape your grace

…And you blow the introduction
in some "chase-the-dawn" hotel
wingless wires just stun tradition
and you want the car to turn around
the room protected by some shadow locks
that melt upon awakening
disappearing present occupants
leave tell-tale handprints on the glass
I'm never gonna let you go

I thought it was you
I thought it was you
crush the life out of a dragonfly
and throw it in the Hudson
I'm trying to sink
to catch truth at the bottom
it's the end of every stylized day without you
can't visit my love
can't visit the mainland
rust on the broken wheels
all buckled into silence
I thought it was snow
instead it was flies

…And curled around the desperate
is the vine that chokes the stonework
and it plays on your affections
and it strangles to perfection
the ghost of everybody count
is trapped inside confessions
and the rogue detectives
from the ether solve just why the sadness lies so low

I'm never gonna let you go
I'm never gonna let you go

A million tiny wings that slander gravity
just like braille against the sun
that never settles on a meaning
save the full stop of the carrion
between the monologues of insects
listless veins ascend like trees
just for the chopping down of rotten fruit

MALEKKO

Fate Won't Conduct

The mist of the minimal
translates as an animal
the force of a wave that splits
you wait to discover it
you lie like a christ in sulphur
genetically drowned at birth
you're going to give all your force to the enemy

Afraid of a close-knit time
secluded and serpentine
through ruins of surrounded words
they sound like a maze of birds
you stand like a shadowed Venus
genetically cut from stone
you're going to give all your force to the enemy

When fate won't conduct
you wake / self-destruct
you dig before you drive
the sand comes alive

Oceans drain on roads completely
marble will disintegrate
biblical the will we question
blast the corpses from the gate

Cadence and Landscape

Lifting levelhalf-life is not a life
swords crossed / silence

x on your listless eyes
versus-closure
sand vanish when you wake

Cadence and landscape
blindness and dissidence
song is insolvent
will is insistent mirrors in winter
voices in tangents
that shine through the last words
and vanish in sand

Beyond frameless
blood signal loud as sun
closed off conditions
sucked back to the front
dissident blindness
grows past impossible

Last to Fall

A storm worth stealing
no mass appeal
to drive a process
afraid to prove
too far from facile
too close to crave
that time is latent
these words are spent

Last to fall repeat fall

No dust to settle
no flame to fan
ashamed to show it

too late to fall
the sound keeps growing
you stare too long
above the ground level
against the wall

I'm Slowly Breathing, Listen

I'm slowly breathing listen
I don't want to pull the bricks from the building
I carried the disciples to deposit them
a turn of the screw

A hymn to the artillery
a poisoned lure
positioned as such
I'm slowly breathing listen
you can follow
without having to touch

Lake drained: innocence framed
a proper send off and service
aloof guards when the road is hard
you don't have to be scared to be nervous
I'm slowly breathing life into an army forged
from puppets and dolls legs
they lope their way to skirmish
of an awkward gait and singular grave

I'm moved by all this majesty
while treason hangs like fruit from a bough
I'm slowly breathing listen
to the litanies I'm living for now

The Whisper in Me

You've got one side of a conversation
and it's garbled, not in a language I know
to push limits to force whispers to death threats
to feel that unstable in a free fall throw

The floods disgraced by their mercurial ending
and the fright is paced through an act of war
and the whispers act by tracing bullets
dragged from flesh wounds where they stood before

Quit walking to the thrust of your own way home
I hear sirens through the whisper in me

BELLS INTO MACHINES

Your Crime Scene My Career

The flightless night—the certainty that separates
a victim from a felony or fail safe
the fluids drip—the M.O. just exsanguinates
the shattered psyche—I came here just to terminate

Be careful—my career
your crime scene—right here
I feed you—I taste you
I know how to waste you

I'll wipe the walls—a bloody technician
the bullet holes—an act of contrition
let's play a game—contaminate the crime scene
and leave a time—you'll never know where I've been

Wretched Little Deity

Dressed up my brain with cross
the wretched deity cause
antipathy fucked by loss
rock of age climbed of course
prayer like a shock to the groin
deity necks employed
rosary stranglehold
you never need to be told

Water to my waist with electric sex
and you never cross wires but you're gonna be next
hang fire from the vine
hang hope from a rope

drink miracle drunk
on disaster faster
never look back from disaster faster
spray the saint's blood
in the language gaps
take another look at the sword you're falling on
burn up the paper of the page your story's on

"Wretched little deity
now you are deceiving me
I suck it up, I'm coming back for more
wretched little god of mine
filthy pantomime
in servitude I'm comin' back for more"

And what if you forgive at last?
Wretched loud/wretched fastwretched loud/wretched fast
wretched loud/wretched fast
wretched loud/wretched fast

Drugs, infidelity and worshipdrugs, infidelity and worship
drugs, infidelity and worship
drugs, infidelity and worship

Ordinary Fascist

Ordinary fascist fits between you and me
indoctrinates banalities and screams out disease
I love him for his facelessness
his toxic eye speech
on TV manifestos
manifest out of reach

Ordinary fascist / deepest lies ever told
an ordinary warzone / you come in from the cold

and underneath America you're trying to show
as ordinary as the loaded weapon you hold

It's a perfect day for marching and I'm here to collect
a continent of militants and steal that respect
I brainwash with asphyxiation shaped like a war
and make my little soldier boys
come begging for more

Now everyone's a fascist and they hide underneath
devices and technology can't bring them relief
instead they torch society and burn it back down
an ordinary fascist with both boots on the ground

Missions

Into the sea
we're gently free
certain, as souls in the tide are surrounded
lip synching prayers
no one is there
no one to witness our lives when they counted

Missions they mean nothing
missions they're a waste
when I can't have you I grow colder
I'm standing in the desert
I'm standing at your door
when I can't have you I grow colder

Back to the beach
barefoot and lost
hold fast your laugh as the moon it engulfs us
mist is a gift
to love on the outside

don't need nobody to be there to help us

Close by your hands
you witness a flame
it comes from my heart to ignite my redemption
next to your lips, a secret, it soars
watch as we witness it's fall and ascension

ATF Shadow

Risk is running in government shapes
the more you say, the more it escapes
the law ain't risk, the risk ain't law
one more bullet, one more door
electric witch hunt, scan your wrist
prints are added to endless list
walk in the shadow of an ATF play
sirens scream where agents stay

ATF shadow—lock all the doors
don't have anywhere else to go
can anyone hear me as the radar screams hard
ATF shadow—play let down your guard

The fifth one back is the van to watch
smile on the face of the driver's forced
silence shoots from the radar to the road
sucked from a message in elaborate code
the fifth one forward is blocking our path
in a separate life I'd probably laugh
in the ATF shadow play, shadow of a gun
shadow of death in the shadow of the sun

I got one on my back, another one on my back

Machine Gun Odessa

You're not quite dying
and you're not quite dead
your fingers move around the trigger head
the blood-soaked telegrams arrive at last
communion with power surges
from the past

Machine gun Odessa
where we can slip right through the sand and run

The fog is anchored to the frigid ground
your ears lie waiting for that C-4 sound
an execution and an exit wound
I would have told you but I fell too soon to a

Machine gun Odessa
where we can slip right through the sand and run

Sweet Life in Soaring Light

It's never quite dawn
so what am I supposed to do?
The millions of answers, they're screaming
but they never come through
you know I try to relate
but my love makes the poor soul whisper
behind tenement walls
all but shrouded in shame when I kissed her, oh no

Sweet life in soaring light
why do you cast your shadows so?
I'm reaching for a taste of the permanent
still I have no place to go

When I cruise at this height
I run the risk of never returning
these secret altitudes
landscapes
echoes of yearning and yearning
your pulse, it is perfect
and it beats in the shape of a song
but it keeps me awake
and it's kept me that way for too long, oh no

Sweet life in soaring light
why do you cast your shadows so?
I'm reaching for a taste of the permanent
and still I have no place to go
the sweet dreams that you perspire
leave a misprint on your skin
the sweet life in soaring light
and the mysteries therein

All these shadows of birds
are upon you as they migrate myths
you wave your arms in the air
and you shriek
and they bite your wrists
too much blood in a pattern
the arcs in the air I breathe
I'm not used to betrayal
so I pick up my things and leave

Video of Slaughter

Another subject in the video of slaughter
strapped to a bomb
or just a sucker in the crosshairs
a holy war unholy digital repentant

another subject in the video of slaughter

Slow down, I found a digital version of the truth
it's outrageous:
boot boys are praying and they're getting their message out loud
on these pages
crippled with static communication
stagger to the world
between airwaves
the video whispers through the teeth of a martyr too late
there's no life saved

Slowdown: on the fingers of a love song
a mystic militia
all the miracles have gone wrong
look at the flock as they record it
on their cell phones
it must be the wisdom that we've waited for for so long

For now I'm just a messenger, locked in the world of plain sight
I know something
I scrape manifestoes off power lines and spray them on walls
it's just one thing
the roar of the righteous, the ricochet risks
in these caves
it's like hunting
the shadows are credible connected to digital ghosts
we're still wanting

Still wantingstill wanting
still wanting
still wanting

FINI TRIBE

FINI TRIBE

An Evening with Clavichords

Evening will come and with its equivalence
no tethered animal would fear to coax
they ask of us favours we cannot fulfil
they ask after us and we smile

Course and condition a trial for fenceless fields
we'll go further, we'll go for the green
a sickly salivation for future fears

Draw pictures of me, pasadena!
Shock me with reason and again we can try
the skin touches
and I can intrude no further

Bring me bring me my tongue on a plate
tease me with my own blurred vision
a phosphorescent shade on a weeping tree
a thorn in the flesh for me

I, the ornate, the latest fate
I have forsaken solitude for you, for you

Backwards and Forwards We Lean

Unquestioning undaunting,
the silence of language
throws tears of strangled language
through corridors of conflict
compromise is useless
when decisions are taken

freeze in your tracks
there's no turning back
even if you believe in the facts based on lies
you can't base your life on an all faithless faith
laughter is one thing
they say that it's good for the soul
laughter is one thing
they say that it's good for the soul

Backwards and forwards we lean
one thought is because of it all
the pilgrimage shifts through a dream
abhorrent meticulous green

A language afraid of the light
an era is ending tonight
the liquid is dry in between
oh backwards and forwards we lean...

Cathedral

Up with night
and with others who believe in this night
another situation lost
I will always be your host, always be your host
pushing it over we said
up with night
up with night
up with night
up with night

Like old wood
translucent and planning within
effervescent and mumbling
you shall effervesce forever

pushing it over
pushing it over
up with night
up with night
up with night
up with night

And what of the festival of night?
Ecstatic tribe rise to fever pitch at midnight
tapping the source at the source
step above a rainless tempest
contained beneath all words in frozen years
transparency is subordinate
silent, moving within
cobalt blue eyes of night disease
stars die of alcohol poison:
like parasites on absolution
genetic magnificate featclaustrophobic of open space
a thousand tribal eyes dissolving the moon with a stare
it was as if we had left the earth!
Our liquid cleansing the parasite soil
our faces and our legs bathed in the liquid light
of the festival
and we reacted on instinct alone
tears and semen speckled the darkest of the gems at our feet
still warm

De Testimony

Serpents are choking,
where violence grows,
dden collapsing,
uncertainty grows,
heaven and sea,

sticking to me.

Oh, for the sight
of your city in flames,
cleansing and purging
the sick from the sane,
you should have known that the
fire was divine,
making your life
the most holy of crimes
you made a mess—
all for the best...

In my mind's eye,
there's a place I should be,
dreaming forever,
of heaven and sea,
thanks to the sun,
burning as one.

Goose Duplicates

The water ran cold, I'm decapitated
hands extend where skin is slated
grins bearing mouths
mouths bearing grins
avoiding all contact
we're riddled with sins

Wait for encouragement
wait for the wind to drop
your answer creates the hell
anxiety now compels

Look for a straw to clutch

die in the longest touch
axe to the easel there
in line with symbolic hair

Anxiety is cyclic
two-fold geese deceit
ideas dormant
lay to rest the hungry fear
installations buried here!

The water ran cold
the water ran cold
bitter the thoughts are hard to hold

Grins bearing mouths
mouths bearing grins
avoiding all contact
we're riddled with sins

Wait for encouragement
wait for the wind to drop
your answer creates the hell
anxiety now compels

Look for a straw to clutch
die in the longest touch
axe to the easel there
in line with symbolic hair

Idiot Strength

Deface and replace
the empty mind
with unholy swords of strength,
captive adults—sickening wrecks,

bed of ill repose,
catholic sex,
behold, we are at the threshold
of idiot strength.

Half the mind is hammer mad,
a diseased robotic function,
and flesh/mechanical makes idiots weep
faith without instruction.

It's so indicative of a puppet life,
hate completes the deficit
in the adult mind.

All pain's abandoned
and the faith dilates,
accusations stumble
from that last embrace

Solitude and servitude,
I hope you understand,
you can't resist to be
raped and twisted and warped
by your fellow man,

You can suck your own cock
if you cut it off,
hack! hack! hack!
you'll never look back.

Me and My Shadow

Because you're always there,
I've never got to know you very well,
you lose—what you gain you lose,

beyond the shadow of a doubt,

This time I know for sure!
Effervescent and mumbling!

Correct me if I'm wrong,
but I believe your spit and image,
decided by a sun that's set at dawn,
beyond the shadow of a doubt,
a curse or a blessing?
Me and my shadow standing flat.

Once more, time's on our side,
take a chance,
take a risk,
play for time,
a curse or a blessing?
Made of rubber and metal…
call me,
mind over matter,
bent over double

The Constant

The edge is thin
and only those who cross between activities
paint pleasure pure on baited flesh
abrupted behind the mesh

Here comes the pulse, profanity and greed

Lapse like an angel
from edge to courage
biting back decay
we constantly display

a wanton curse persuasion can't delay
a truth that was a million chains too late

The vital touch that warm wet eyes deny
instinctively we play
in principle we pray
for innocence about to fall from grace
here the edge is thin,
my skin is far too thin
so slight to break
it makes the energy
count out time and again

The constant crack of chains unbroken years away
deceptive to the point that made them fade away
heaven, I'm in heaven long before I leave the room
edge closer as we fall into our own
the unknown

We're Interested

Cross a wide canal in your dreams
reach the other side and pass over again
and the murky underneath
shall start to come out
we're the people stay underneath
aha my stomach folds and folds again
and turns into a wreath
cross a wide canal in your dreams

We're interested in ambience
the pattern it makes
a gently moving lattice
the king of your mind
we're interested in knowing your kind

And waking's not enough when you're evading amnesia
we're interested in time: the hours that you keep
we're interested in all that is sublime
and those that never draw but cross the line

Move a little turn a little show us how little you are
move a little turn a little show us how little you are
make amends
make a mess on the floor
in a gently waking moment

COLLABORATIONS
AND
UNUSED LYRICS

WITH PAUL BARKER

Evangelical Sound Barrier

You can't even take the fucking rubbish out
without someone looking at you
trying to see where you live
and going through your garbage afterwards
looking for little numbers
and little fucking notes
little fucking clues
a bandage with dried blood
or a ripped-up brochure
that probably wasn't yours
to begin with

Through misted waste
the sordid and silent place
ignored and the blamed alert
other adjectives you never heard
the shocking style
now breaking evangelical
and falling on fictitious swords
other adjectives you never heard
they walk when shocked
surrounded by some soldier talk
in luminous and lusted air
sound barrier too high for prayer

Where is this treason that
locked eyes on bloody revolutions
trying to find comfort as we move to the left
somewhere moved to the left
as we slice the evangelical sound barrier

One misses the west and it's winter...
(bloody revolution)

Heavy Water

We climb at fly to a beauty thing
we don't have time to acquire
the signal's path to paralysis
the shadowed voice on the wire
the clusters make mazes of hillsides
they roll down chances and risks
our fate levitates from the water
the truth sucks the strength from our wrists

We're cloned in motion and murdered
the parallels rent to redeem
the flow like a spillage to paradise
with no heavy water between

The fences and merchants of menace
the physical drowning elite
they flow like a spillage to breathless
washed upon shores dead at our feet

We're begin to drown where we thought
heavy water, dead at our feet

The first of ice is fantastic
it's frail like measured mistakes
it climbs in the worst of your waking
looks for unconscious to take

The freedom controls condescension
it blasts from the walls broken age
deserted by merchants of menace

it blasts from the wall's broken stage

WITH BLACK NEEDLE NOISE

I'll Give You Shape

The cloth perspires again
it stirs our night time
my silent friend
a surge like never before
it craves the movement
you can't ignore

I'll give you a shape
I'll give a verse to read for heaven's sake
the message is solar, then the whisper fades
the lover has form
reverse the light
from corresponding storm
the path obscured and the pages torn

Now vapour defines our peace
we tried flinching backwards
but there is no release
we still stir magic
with these whispering cords
trace tightly your outline
where there are never words

I'll give you a shape
it might define this place
when it gets late
the maze is empty
but it's still our home
I keep feeling midnight
but the day outside is open wide

the mirror blinds where I come from

I'll give you a shape
within the sleepless fields
the fingers steal
the estuary diver
with his wings for soul
and you feel the movement
are these solid waves upon your face?
Do you feel the kiss through the misted wall?

WITH FRONT LINE ASSEMBLY

The Spitting Wind

Replacing all the air
you replace until there's nothing there
you makeshift suffocate
the words before the meaning
then the voice is heard, oh, the voice is heard

The voice is a stream of pain
like from a falling plane
revolves round the world again
the texture still isn't right
cowers from a hunter's light
makes for a stranger to sleep with tonight

To rest here is asinine
between electric lines
forgive me: instantly chilled to the bone

We trawl through shame
through lover's names
through the backlit scars
through the frigid wars
and we burn our crimes (and we burn our crimes)
between electric lines (between electric lines)
say a prayer for nothing (say a prayer for nothing)
here I am a ghost (here I am a ghost)
a shadow lingering (yes it's lingering)
I am a toxic host (just a toxic host)
no sense imagining (imagining)

The voice is a shock to you

all made of ice, and through
the pages wet with no one's story never true
it climbs through your open pores
behind your distant doors
distorts the age you never claimed
that was your own
 the frayed pages hide the end
therein, the plot descends
to whispers
barely heard above the spitting wind

Rules

Yes, so the message goes
like an insect in its death throes
a magic carpet ride to hell
then back to here with time to tell
a metal scar on every face
we walk to a forbidden place
where dirty water cleans the soul
we pour into another hole

Here comes a secret delivery
all aboard the reason why
a broken-down discovery
the rules, the rules do not apply

I'm half blind and I'm losing
a picture that is out of control
I'm lying on the ground but I'm moving
a prison being built round my soul

Under a concrete sky
barricades begin to rise
sun and stars begin to fall
a sonic boom condemns us all
decapitated soldiers fight
and ministers control the light
in leaking gas we bake our flesh
and in the air we fight for breath

Craze

Nailed against another wall
light or dark—break and start
idiot could play the part
make it mine—pain and crime
fading light—other signs
take it back—crowbars crack
break it down—remain intact
there's nothing like giving the game away
all the people are feeling the same today
take a hammer and break a bone for me
there's nothing like giving the game away

Blame

Secrets insane
halfway to paradise
against every grain
prayers burn a hole thru baby
always the same
walk-stalking nights like nothing leveled the same
it's always the same

Wake every brain
three steps to heaven
and you'll fall back again
thru drilling holes for air
now breathe in the blame
sleep-walking nights are useless lives to be drained
always the same

Couldn't be denied
before the secret died

Ikons

Lead base for the Holy Ghost
inebriated leather host
a loaded, bladed, silent pain
will nail you to the world again

The dead are implicated
implied but never stated
carve me out those other words to live by
to live by

Strychnine starts the bleeding dark
metals aging
birth and mark
shards of empty battle grey
poisoned beasts are out to play

The dead are implicated
implied but never stated
carve me out those other words to live by
to live by

Yeah mine's sterilized as well
I never used it can't you tell
it's small enough to hide in your
favourite icon's mouth

A loaded, bladed, silent pain
will nail you to the world again

The dead are implicated
implied but never stated
carve me out those other words to live by
to live by

WITH MESHELL NDEGEOCELLO

Rapid Fire

It was a time too tired for rapid fire
and cages spilled their guts into the street
spying on lovers, solving puzzles
trying to breathe some life into the heat
may the storm dissolve your presence
or your legend for a second while it fills your past
say you're sorry for absolving
say you're mad because you couldn't make it last

And suddenly I was unconscious
trying to pull something from this
I looked at claws instead of birds
and chased the meaning from the words

Seemed like a million lording over levelled songs
music whispered out of comas, incomplete
the notes are all fractured, the bars are decayed
carve that serenade to a lover's leap
may a smile convert your figure to a flow
or a river drowning fingerprints to snow
say you'll swim because the sinking requires too much thought
say you'll breathe because in leaving you have nowhere else to go

And there were frights we would endure in squalid hours
and ways of passage through to morning without dreams
nonstop fiction, all those tattle tale eyes
cut the words out to hear the spaces in between
spirits ushered, stark naked back to cage
flightless envoys, scarred by human rage
fleeting keys, quick to dazzle / slow to lock

fleeting gasps, in squalid hours mesmerize the shock

And suddenly I became airborne
an acrobat my resolve torn
I wondered loud of where to land
I did not try to understand

Never Still Water

Don't slide,
into the background
where silence is sacred
you'd never believe it–
a throat in the darkness
sings of perilous hearts
too loud for a prayer
too long for a warning
too short for confession
too quiet for love

Stones thrown,
mystery sins and second skin
too frightened to touch it
we're here to persuade you
to cover your tracks
you sit through survival
you sit through a sermon
you sit through a side show
you sit through romance

All you ever want of me
is written on water, never still water
all you ever seem to see
is written on water, never still water
I might decide I might decide

never still water
I might decide I might decide
never still water

Sometimes
a scythe through the flower bed
when nothing is said
a silence so tragic
it mirrors a murder
the wages of lust
it's time for redemption
it's time for an answer
that's written on water
that I might decipher

Sometimes,
the danger so close
midnight whispers of lovers
my back to your background
I'm trying to find you
and make you read back
all these words on the water
these words don't make sense
they're ever revolving
the ripples unwoken

Shopping for Jazz

Shoppin' for jazz,
if the big girls don't mind
to clap or just snap my fingers—I'm tryin' to decide,
the world is just pushin'
got a flow of its own
riding the tide of last night,
and it's never alone.

The falling notes, a landslide
picture perfect, love is nowhere,
I was silence,
you were breathless,
shoppin' for jazz...

Browsin' the walls,
like a solo in shreds,
a flight in a tattered landscape,
I'll sing you instead,
I'm lookin' for motion,
'cos honey, I move...like the air from a thunder condition
with nothing to prove

Afraid of sweetness shocking
coat my skin in promised passion,
seek direction,
then reflection,
shoppin' for jazz...

WITH THE JOY THIEVES

This Will Kill That

I try to maintain,
a victim of my own lucidity
and when I try to stay sane
all the madness just crawls right out of me
when I throw on the light
my body in relief/it's clinical
a corpse dying of fright
the movement in the mirror is minimal

Bet you never thought
that this will kill that
bet you never thought
bet you never thought
I never thought
you're trying to do what?
Make this one kill that
trying to do what
you were always scared of

To focus is hard
for lips that never move to communicate
and I'm always on guard
the object of the force to terminate
it's a throw away life
my body and my thoughts just vaporize
and I'm covered in bites
by a madness that remains still weaponized

A maze that's mine
a blade so fine

bet you never thought...
I never thought...

Trying to do what you were always scared of...

UNUSED LYRICS

The Opium Glove Puppet

Three blind mice
and the opium dice,
six spots of poison
beneath a reaction to light,
grab your own gravity
blame it on hunger and stains,
force-fed on sunburst,
repeat me in one fourth of rain.

Heaven on horseback!
Why must I risk my neck
just for a game?
So be it.
I'm full of it.

Shamefaced shines
to the quick of surprise,
bleed open marvels,
in secret to burn the first prize,
live the next chapter,
repeat after me and be calm.
A flame beyond reason,
a glove puppets hands can do harm.

Heaven on horseback!
Why must I risk my neck
just for a game?

Fantastic and fake,
the waves start to break,

don't look at it,
throw a six,
anything,
Mama, why does it hurt?

With corresponding cave-dog eyes,
and never known secret signs,
the breed of reactions rise,
the way is only up and so much more,
counting six up to a thousand
and back to four.
Cry yourself a river,
when you cheat,
you make a sorry move,
when you cheat the chances are,
there is something trivial left
you feel you have to prove,
all of this and more
takes us down from six to four.

Fantastic and fake
the waves start to break.

Still Born

The moon burns holes where my tears used to roll,
she conjures up a storm
and another child is born,
the mother, she just passed away
her young life stolen and grey,
the taste of honey on her moist lips,
that suffocate
between child bearing hips.

Let me tell you of agony, father

with what you feel for your child,
her screaming dependency
cuts the storm like a knife
as you hold her to the moon
in blind love
what witness craves lunacy
all on this night?
So wet her dying lips
outstretched your arms kiss heaven
for lack of life
this child will be given
unto mercy
and the brazen tides,
hold her to the breast of the storm,
kiss the lips that pray her born,

Let me please unsex you father,
remove from your brow
the question of intensity
you felt that day,
where in the bed you did lay,
and placed your hands upon her breasts,
and licked her warm and tragic flesh,
and pulled her to your figure's length,
to feel your sorrow, and your strength,
let me watch you lick her,
and relish in her moisture,

Your eyes and mind are closed,
desire and deathwish grows,
all hidden from decision,
until the child is born,
and we die in the storm.

I cover my face with my hands

I cover my face with my hands,
because again, I am too scared to look,
The deepest threat is the lock
on my door.
It oscillates.

And silently I look through the keyhole,
and try to decide
which line it is
that I should cross.
The edge is shrinking
and like so many distant tides before it
swelling its breast towards the moon.
Oh, to wash these gems up on one more shore.
Before I die.
Oh, to crush these stones with the weight of my bitterness,
and send the black sand with a whirlwind into the eyes of those
who cheated me. Not me,
I cover my face with my hands
and I wait until the wind subsides
and I hold up an element of truth,
so I can find my way back to my emptiness.

I can climb into my own emptiness
and use the silence to cut myself open,
remorse, like a sacrificial slaughter
spills violently onto the floor,
and I scream loudly at myself
for being so weak
I stare loudly at myself
I wake myself up with a shock
I kill myself to sleep every night
I kick myself towards my own submission.

I cover my face with my hands
I cover my face with my hands
still shrinking, the water's face is furrowed, then calm,

My brow aches from one too many cuts.

Stone Cut Scissors

Stone cut scissor
to melt the hangman's stay,
I stood my ground
to drown on judgment day,
I'll build my own cage,
leave me lying here,
been stung too many times
before this year.

I stepped on glass between the two of us,
of us each one out of reach,
passed me by and never knew of us,
and took away my power of speech.

The sane betrayed me with their therapy
I never knew who to believe,
and then I stole hope from telepathy,
gave up finding ways to leave.

Riding time out like the ghost of you,
I move on dawn with crippled sight,
the threat of comfort cuts the day in two,
I hold my own and start to fight.

Forget I ever promised anything
of course I lied, of course I lied, you smiled—

that shadow shattered everything,
your darkness hung in chains outside.

I'm gonna brace myself for injury,
throw dreams like caution to the wind,
blame your darkness for my sanity,
burn the place where dreams begin.

Burn it deeper,
so much deeper than before,
wake the sleeper,
when we both can sleep no more.

Stone cut scissors
cut the day in two
solid gold,
the ghost of you.

Borstal

The ground switch is talking,
connecting vice to the stars,
where are all those sleepers,
blacked out in stories cry,
I would move you,
they're decking land's end,
in a swallowed second,
removing agendas by the age.

Don't know how to move you,
or should I ever move you?
Down in the waders ground—
no land
no substance,
no war for land,

I shouldn't say that you moved first,
down in the waders land,
all these breaknecks,
can sweep you away,
away from the mind-fields,
that put you there first
away from the giants
that rained on us last,
a moving picture,
the crowd leaves,
in need of a scribbled saviour,
"Party of one,
the borstal is waiting"
show me my room,
and show me the middle of anxious,
party of one,
you are moved to mistakes,
six black spars amount to daylight,
it stops when the motion breaks,
don't stray me,
don't stray me,
party of one,
your lies in a line,
starving and soaking,
you brandish your belt to the wind
don't start,
don't start,
don't start me at all.

Millionaire

Do you believe me now?
They have taken it away from you,
all the blind drunks are raining down,
laughing, listless,

If you had hands you'd pick up that weapon,
and you would use it on who you love most,
if you had legs you would kick in that locked door,
but your motions are crippled and forced,
and all the heaving sobs you ever faked,
draped on a pair of cold shoulders,
knowing nods, at last, you're cold
do you believe me now?
You are being robbed of your right
to destroy your insides,
the pill blackouts are catching up,
with their mocking strangled sounds,
their black tongues are slobbering
in between words about you.
Did you walk through that fog,
to emerge like a saint?
Or did you sit yourself down
in the vain hope the vapour would drown you?
Do you believe me now?
In silence,
when there are no more lies to hear,
and every other cable
is choking
with talk about you.

Minder

What climbed the walls to fall?
Be they walls—sound shaking,
was it you?
Carved its new point
from our wonder,
from our fear,
a new place of worship
and we arrive near.

His grief arrives slowly,
on crests of a major limitless dare,
how brave to breathe solely!
Fathomless air.
Collapse needs a science
to cancel out spells
it did spread.

Untitled

There is hard stone frost and forest,
lie drake left awake,
black staring bird,
throw belch for pincer children,
children end forget,
clawing need reject,
a focus of farther thirst,
a tongue dry hard stone and frost,
baby-squeak claws adopted,
rich is skin,
shallow is bone.

On Passing Amongst You

Scant eyes, scarcely literal,
one or two of you,
faked special,
of foreign or blind measures,
half-dropped slippery heart,
on passing among you,
tired,
sanguine eyes, still yet,
strangely aware
makes their way
to be over

the shock of amongst.

You would surge #1

And creatures moved no less
than afforded them
by weightless saviours,
bleed-fleets of brevity,
lie stacked and strangle,
on threatened ages…
All injured false
with backward pulse
you would surge inside.

Collapse

What world filled with black
instead of sedatives?
Which point of collapse
brings fever and liquid metals
into hatred's heart.
Don't cry for me, dear heart,
for I won't let you open the gate
of my wretched secret.
No tears for me dear heart!
for I will never let you expose yourself
to the naked truth.

Where one hand holds another softly
the other grips a knife,
where one life collapses into nothing
the other cannot be moved to anything.
What life so tormented collapses
twisting and black as pitch?
Though deep the hole there are no sides to the wall,

tortured dreams will climb downwards
demented in
no-motion substance.

My nails will break my spine.

Not through Glass

Throwing a rock to see,
a rock through injured spaces,
is it me you're looking for?
I've seen stranger things before,

Your aim seemed dislocated,
until negative divides,
and the undressing of your wounds,
became addictive all too soon,

Deciders spoke in circles
to mediate the flames—
the prayers ending now,
and not through glass too
not through glass too.

The limits were boarded fast
and your blood grew unlit circles,
like the passages we drained
in praise of everything we blamed.

Instilling a likeness
of some city light disguise
could short, and break the targets back,
and leave assassins still intact.

To bribe a born accomplice

to look you in the eye
and say he cared for you
and not through glass, too
not through glass too.

A distance of broken parts
blurs the image of madness black,
invades the confines of your grasp,
to find a lie that wouldn't last.

It was freezing the night we clawed
for ideas to make us stable,
and we unlocked a million doors,
we've done stranger things before.

The zeal of hypocrites
brings home demand to you,
a gang of strangers spitting,
not through glass, too.

No known wingspan

Low and east to the moon
did the forest speak itself quietly?
A million night growls
on city slates,
on city slaves,
harmony crashed in a winter.

Yours not is harmony,
yours is not…
fire me
breathe entire
walking/fractured.

Loudest to the moon,
it's imaginary wingspan intact for now
it is imaginary,
it is flapping lies,
to the fighters,
grateful's finest moment,
relived through yours.

Untitled

I saw a fraction
of bird-like murky diamonds,
it did pass this way,
it joined flag staffs,
like no nation would,
in a cackle of feathered air,
it's forced eyeless might
in staggered future,
a figure of air,
did lift
a measure of wind carried over,
from last night,
a withered gut,
in exchange for dry worm.

Comfort and Joy

If you could be right here with me,
we'll call it a Sunday afternoon
and your world's still asleep for awhile
what's more, your dream is intact from last night
it's left marks on your smile
no creation is left unattached
when you wake out of breath,
I see your mercy explode with the myth

that it's all you have left,

Come one, come all
I heard you call
witness the end of an era where sanity crumbles and falls
the mantra's maliciously crucified imbecile falls
so what? I'm not bound by patience
or bleak apparitions no more,
just think, your dreams could ignite
like a beast and come claw at your door,

Who says I gave a fuck for your sanity?
A scathing attack on a mind that's intact and perverse.

Witness the fall to the blackest hole
T minus ten, I hear the voice scream again and we hide
under surrogate wombs, under make believe rooms
and the night
point the looking glass up to the sky and pretend not to see
and if you don't believe in pain
I suggest you all think again and then freeze,

Survived by none and renounce the sun
nail your temper to the wall, detonate, sit down and wait
endure the downfall of reason, your family burnt at the stake
nail your temper down harder this time and you'll never grow old
waiting for comfort and joy to come in from the cold.

Die like wind, a promise

Fire invested,
so much more
to bleed you down,
the missing stranger,
a starving angel;

mother, I'm lost and found,

You make me frantic,
but you're so warm,
you die at dawn,
and I'm so grateful,
forever fallen,
don't get me wrong.

Between the pages so much more to count,
but getting there it seems so hard,
I'll leave a message just as soon as I am found,
forgive me friends, I'm thrown apart.

A promise leaving,
I heard your breathing next to mine,
you sold a shadow,
to unknown forces,
how they laughed unkind!
A favourite painting,
beautifully burning,
for us light!
Don't fake your blindness,
you are so kind as to
give up your sight.

A hanging gift beneath a dying star,
don't reach too high!
You'll burn your hand!
We'll save the next one just to ease your troubled mind,
we stop tonight,
when the flames are fanned.

The Giddy Horses

The giddy horses,
the past life intentions,
the naming without blaming,

See that high crossed wire!
See that dying judge of distance!
See that laughing matter!
The mark of energy, bitten eyes of the month, smooth,
like racing to rescue,
moss scored ink walls, can't react until
the prisoner's injured...
mask of crawling goal.
The giddy horses!
The past life intentions!
The naming without blaming!
See that low arched winder,
acts as a homing device,
crossed maker of praise,
a would be judge of distance,
mist of antique wounds,
figures stuck and winding,
draped like a soldiers incentives,
flock to the edge to look,
wind blew them to the stations of heaven,
makers of mist...
the giddy horses,
the past life intentions,
the naming without blaming

Doggy walk/mock

Brings stacks back home
to his Dad,

sticks in bundled forties,
the moron,
mocked by dog walked,
faltering stick he is thrown,
cross-flawed boomerang stare,
cracks right between fatty eyes,
look, tamper in circles running,
cut syrup-blood oozing,
the child's vacant face-place,
mocked by circling doggy,
what does dad look on in
simple rustic lusty rage,
I would fear yes!
I would wipe it all the blood
with muddy cake hands,
clumsy two thick fingery,
like to probe open flaps,
of grey and swollen flab-flesh,
just for a minute black probing,
worms infected fat.

Untitled

Where did the winds missile end
all of us?
No wind or water green and supreme,
the catch,
the squeal guarded victims resignation,
or motor functioned arrest victory,
there can a birds-eye slowly feel,
or fail to rise its bony beak as
it splits another surface to heal.
There can a birds' claw peel inward,
from misery too late to miss
its ghost prey,

like walls bleed in fathoms,
growing to old ones and shrinking,
with a whimper back to ragged birth,
an island, a skinny flaw,
a frail moon or anemic Jupiter
dusts the planet for hidden treasure.

The Song

Late clients will draw the truth,
out of strangling stares,
reminding reign,
flee the thousand downs,
a measured cover up—ungraded,
aches for your breeding,
canonized—he fakes another alliance,
the counter is way off—
go start your song again,
re-write the words, for worried wakes and dies,
while you sleep,
drink from the roof you did thatch
with the neck of your song,
go sing your song,
she's an old girl,
given to shapeless,
involved in a storm—
1000 down, 1000 down,
go start your storm,
show the old girl worth
unsteady, instead,
a break in this lateness
will be the death of you—
awake and deflated,
the death of you,
wait, wait.

Go sing your song,
for the emptiest time,
fill your breast,
so the old girl will shine.

The Morning After

I woke with broken age,
to spoil another page,
you cannot blame the morning after.
Significant blood will drain,
all over your face like rain,
don't blame it on matricide,
don't blame it on love the morning after.

I'm still gonna hide from you,
submerged and destitute,
give a sign if you feel betrayed,
broken promises never made.

Soaking bodies, second time,
bring to me what is not mine,
leave outside my door to waste,
climb on board my violent face,
you can't correct the morning after,

A force of injury,
unspoken imagery,
you can't contain the morning after,
the lines on a hand appear,
in a broken hemisphere,
don't call on the guiding light,
don't call on your friends the morning after,

I'm still gonna hide from you,

submerged and destitute,
give a sign if you feel betrayed,
broken promises never made,

We'll drown birds in dream retreats,
prey on men we'll never meet,
hanging gifts for hungry hearts,
grateful, blind, and blown apart,
don't plan to wake the morning after,
shadow forces laughed unkind,
stifled breathing next to mine,
hide a clock from the doctor's eye,
wet and wordless, paralyzed,
don't turn on the light the morning after.

Rondo

Written to be sung alternately by two people.

If cold could just leave my arms there,
well, a moment to revive,
will ensure we can arrive
to just stand and stare.

I'm not light enough
gravity's easy—
don't force me to
push my arms into the air.

Here's that sound again,
turning round again
a fleeting "implore me"
decides the direction tonight.
This evening's confessions make ice the vice,
and no one sleeps harder than I do,

this freezing is paradise.

In walks circumstance,
you're farther away now,
a trick of the time you should know.
I was walking to music
that somebody sings to me
through the dark leafs of my wall,
now, no one can hear me at all.

All this evenings requests
left in piles by the bandstand
just waiting for someone to play…

Mocking bird, Dog bird

Look past a man;
past winter's own hand…
bleak, free,
the mutt in her majesty,
she-bitch, and bringer of prey…
succour and soaker,
disguise becomes
the louder yelled.

The park done on purpose,
what we done dreamed,
of fledgling-grey nocturnes,
battle glass feathers
on unkempt walls,
bullfrog in startled turns, burns,
childish mistake
of nature, buggered,
breathing cobwebs of fruit
fell and splashed open

cast like a shadow
where germs did freeze,
they are hanging dead birds
off the sycamore trees.

And mind it is mortal,
cracked bone and it shall not fly,
rocking instead like a pigeon head,
bristle tines like a termite trapeze
opened up yellow escaping boil,
bride, be devoured,
yellow-river eyes,
bird dog eyes,
hanging chick,
look! A moment!
Her smiling guise!

Nape

That light was disturbed only by one thing:
the nape of that shadow,
likened to its lateness like spars in water,
the nape of the neck
refused us that shadow,
refused us that shallow,
it is always late afternoon,
always too far beyond
a prayer hour,
too far beyond good as gold,
in afternoon's late drapes
this nowhere could be a garden,
ready to paint a mood on its listeners,
a spar broken as he listens—
no shortage of listeners,
splintered through his shape suit,

and into his anxious skin,
just point to be noticed,
point to distract,
and steal back your love,
late afternoon perfumed,
it riddles your throat
it screams off his shaped suit,
it disturbs,
we listened for prayer hour,
that shall not come
that shall not come
that shall not come,
shallow, come.

Eyetooth

Boys,
here comes another one,
broke frozen, shattered crystal
you point your battered eye mouth
you point to the shore
oh, beckon the shore,
lazy grey drops
in the shuddering sea,
to untie the ballasts,
to create something better than you, boys,
a scythe maintains horizon
an ugly figure does
leave this picture:
your magic is turned upside down,
your magic is poured back into the water,
tired, heaving magic,
drizzling second guess
for the first wave of sleep.

The Letter 'O'

Forgiveness failed us:
that every step taken is an imaginary border,
that you would desert your country and expect blessing,
the weight and force
of lies from your chest,
sacred circles, meridians,
or just the letter 'o'
the exclamation when you learn you are finite,
that you are chipping away at war
hiding away what little you accumulate,
dreaming yourself back
to the coasts you have abandoned,
only to see them crumbling and atrophied,
walls and lighthouses drowning and formless
the perpetual light that remains
a preamble to perpetual storm.

I need to go to this place
and I need to do it all again,
in sorrow, forgiveness and exile,
the path is dripping wet,
the soldiers are listed as exiles,
as pure they can but push it all away,

Sub section lights
a space between dead air and dying ground

Probing edges
like some disqualified expert

A hand that measured life and last mistakes

Forgiveness and exile—I though the sculptures were clear

relief on the hills
by the dykes and the cairns
impassive since bronze age.

20 Hands

20 hands synchronized
in this time torn city's eyes
makes this view seem consumed
somehow paralyzed
and to think that we sink
state of war now hypnotized

Mess with glare instead of blindness and you're going to lose
I guess that fabricates the use of hands
start with slogans made for no one and the crowd will burst
exploding demands the show of hands

20 hands on the wall
trying to climb back to a void
tear the words fear the birds
how d'ya get so paranoid?
And to think it's instinct
every breath has been destroyed

Looks like someone was a witness to a waking world
it seemed so timeless to a nocturne beat
all arms outstretched to make a destination physical
all arms retract when we admit defeat

Silence is the strength of your heaven or hands
and you're never caught leavin'and you're never caught leavin'

Never look back 'cos you can't turn round
and you can't look straightand you can't look straight

and you can't look straight
and you can't look straight

Patricia

Reveal and separate
a world of disclosure
trading entry wounds
for exit stance
river flight of a distance
and the instance
goes horribly wrong
I traded all my braille for broken glass
embracing stranger kills
who destroyed your will
lope through city gates
with ancient light
a decade wide
faceless lines round patrician eyes
up here, all modern efforts die
collection plates a minefield
of minus air.
Reveal and separate
forgiven in our wisdom
we'll come crawling back
to a void commanded by negative moons
where light can't be a magnet
only decades wide
only decades wide
only decades wide
the fractured surface
will connect to persist
the limits of our patience
decided by anti-gods
in weightless angel rooms

the fiction time addicted
to a pry-me-open language
beautific minefield eyes
Patricia, Patricia, Patricia
your horses and your legacy
lined up outside the palace
and shot in cold blood
Patricia, Patricia, Patricia
your blood stains the starving
tattered flag of forces
the mighty wilds of Mongolian winter plain
to mountain suffrage
and no more the ancient light
the shaken end of promise
climbing walls to escape
the godess cramps of withdrawal
sweat stains the size of Pangea
drown counter-whispers
black out endless "could do" lists
with a sweep of my arm
Patricia, Patricia, Patricia
your skull turned into a chalice
brimming with altar wine
in crowded temples
the minds so unopened
as to extinguish
the ancient light
the only thing we have left is this human context.

The Life Model

Moving through the waste
moving through the wires
communicating prayers
diseased empires

is that a wasp on the breeze?
As it falls by degrees
or a bomb that fell?
You know I just can't tell

Implicit the fractured fall
because the life model covers it all
it's a far cry, the stain on your window
but it's a curtain call

Loose, loose, loose
gonna turn the shadow loose, loose, loose

The life model's dead
couldn't pull her from the edge
it's probable she fell
I wish she flew instead
is there a presence in the room?
Because you left too soon
like when a silence fell
you know I just can't tell

The Badlander

Who's that covering the road with shame?
In and out the bleeding sky
the twilight of terrestrials
behold! A mirror flecked with body heat
makes a drain on your resources
and the weakness in dispersed
in my eyes there was a figment of the badlands,
and it spun electric failure
like a map of my contempt
and my dreams were drowned by visions of the badlands
burn the myths bereaved in churches

you will never know

Beckoning to meet the badlander
a name dissolving, systematic saint
and you're never going to beat the badlander
contempt for all the wisdom of restraint

Who's that collecting at the door for debt?
Up and down demolished stairs
the mist of your involvement
look up! A ceiling stained with paraffin
drips betrayal on your candles
flaming nihilist dispersed
by the window was an etching of the badlands
and it made reverse impressions
like a mask of my dissent
and my cuts were opened nightly by the badlands
scar cathedral walls by furnace
you will never know

Run the races on the needles of democracy
the finish line, you never find peace
bleed the badlands into madlands into fantasy
you'll stick it in and never find release

I'm the badlander

Beckoning to meet the badlander
a name dissolving, systematic saint
and you're never going to beat the badlander
contempt for all the wisdom of restraint

Envy in the Headlights

In control of nothing at all
follow your lead with the voice you need
that spot of light on a wretched night
my envy in the headlights overtaking you
that blade of prayer breaks a molten stare
my envy in the headlights overtaking you

We breathe brilliance in the time we kill
and hide the bliss that we condemn
a fallen killer burns the barren air
just like envy in the headlights overtaking you
envy in the headlights overtaking you
envy in the headlights overtaking you
envy in the headlights overtaking you

I feel like wishing you alive was always wrong
it's that envy, it's that envy ah ah ah

But just to pull you off the street where you collapsed
it's that envy, it's that envy ah ah ah

When I sing you to a deeper kind of coma
it's that envy, it's that envy ah ah ah

How to...

How to make the angle silent
within the words of warning
I can convince myself
I couldn't see the surface
I'm gonna dive right in
like with a drowning purpose
I just refuse to swim

(I do it my way)

How to: when you can't feel with your hands
repeat like a staggering man
in a valley of pistols
a metal mist
in the pocket of an alchemist
sets a precedent for modern cluster
on the verge of a whisper

How to bring a "class" to trial
with all the subtext static
upon your open mouths
I couldn't bend the scripture
I'm gonna score it all out
like with a writer's envy
I've got to drown with doubt

In Praise of Yearning

The verses are sung
by a draughtsman drawing on the sea
his numbers and instruments
blurred by perception
they sink through encryption
and flow towards me

I am the mast whose flag blocks the sun
the folly in turning
in praise of yearning
an hour in the ocean
is a lifetime on land
starved of horizons
the mystery widens
the dragnet so drunk

and it asks many questions
you shiver from the breath
you can't catch any messages left
by the draughtsman drowning on islands
positioned and pockmarked
by shadows and caves

In praise of yearning
its ricochet ripples in light
the moment is golden
its clenched fists hang on to the sand
then it falls like a failed constellation
the draughtsman forgot
how to draw on the land
his instruments brittle
from desert neglect
for once in his lifetime
he is late to collect
the chorus of waves
frozen in line

Mister Swansong

Because I'll never sing in English
like the poet that brings this
a seam is split through the city
and the sadness is the electricity
I'm not talking 'bout the motion or the manner
the one that fell in love with your lover's demeanor
I'm not toying with my baby's folly
I'm just electric when I'm melancholy

Deja deja (come and meet my perception)
deja deja (I'm not sticking to a script)
deja deja (and I'm not above a lovesong)

deja deja (if it's written on your lips)

When the light stops ticking
it wasn't meant to be
oh the sentiment is strong
not above a love song
are you a fan of the cryptic?
Because I've got one for you
you see we don't belong
just call me Mr. Swansong

Electric melancholy
and the silk walls of my verse
ticking! Seconds! Every love song
and the timeline is reversed
deja deja
deja deja
deja deja
deja deja

Mr. Swansong lovers, deja deja

Sand Banks

The resurrection at sea
as spirits parade
submerged on sandbanks,
you listen to the shell's heart-worn ballads and eulogies,
half roared at low volume,
the people have been too frightened to swim,
the dead sea had us all humbled at high tide,
leveled at low tide,
rumours of islands
and disappearing craft,
legends of clouds without pity,

and force without mercy,
have brought me here—and now I idle,
the pushing and the shaking of fake equators
has made me become with the sea-all undertow, peaks and troughs,
bully the languid limbs whilst the persistent channels
trespass into yawing vein and usher out panicked blood,
the pores on blue white skin,
eroded to herald in the tempest.
Of all seas, the dead sea
but at least I am here,
at least it can't hurt me,
now it has consumed me.

The City in Your Eyes

Let's put out the fire we're livin' in
ignore the world that's always listenin'
a mission to the city in your eyes,
where lovers like the two of us can hide,
a birthright to uncertainty and fear
will trail us right until we dissappear,
the questions we were asked might set us free
a city in your eyes for you and me

Outside the doors and windows
close with our shadows intact
we move to a world with the wide-open spaces
my love will never look back

Let's destroy the history of pain
ignore the masters, never let them in
it's dawn inside the city of your eyes
the madness and the darkness stay outside
derail the mind from battles that you fought
in case they read it right before you're caught

they'll never step outside our city gates
our minds are closed to them now we've escaped

Streets where we walk with our freedom
skies where our secret's absolved
we'll fly through our city and dance on the rooftops
my love will never look back

These Days Between Storms

You said there was a storm coming
that making plans was not a choice
you drew it on the mist with fingers
erased it with the secrets kept

These days between storms
not a word is said
not a sun is set
when the wane is worthless
I'll turn to you instead

Gone is your fog of reason
your doubt of the altitude
where lovers are freezing
an aerial view of the truth we knew
obscured in the shade for a reason
your stuttering fine print
is gone in an instant
like days between storms

A place between you and your hindsight
don't pretend that it's alright
your love is a landmark
an aerial view of the dreams you drowned
it's there like the frost on your window

it's what you turned into
like days between storms
are years between love
days between storms
years between love

THE STRIP CLUB

REVOLTING COCKS

Stainless Steel Providers

Stainless steel providers
make it obvious—
we like driving the point home,
a hundred thousand vagabond insects
all making a meal out of stainless steel,
you should kick away the watchword
and throw caution to the wind;
remember what it's like
when we are
screaming/dreaming
screaming/dreaming
screaming/dreaming
stainless steel.

Get around, get around, I get around,
when it's time to go,
I'm the first to know,
a parasitic nation
is it good enough for me?
I'll make you a mantra,
from monkeys and carbombs,
beneath,
beneath,
beneath,

Quick locate and detonate
your public enemy,
stainless steel,
believe it's real,
it's all you mean to me,

what's that sound?
What's that sound?
It bleeds efficiency
the way I feel on stainless steel,
and all it does to me.

Stainless steel providers,
another tire, let it catch on fire,
a metal motor mantra
makes you waste the time of day,
you'll sit on a time bomb,
forever and ever,
now breathe…

Can't Sit Still

Temper frayed and sanctified,
delivered up in flames,
no eyes, no grace, no motion,
no mention of the game.

The sweetest flower in the valley,
the sickest joke in the book,
why don't you keep your eyes tightly shut,
'cos I don't want you to look.

If you can't sit still,
you can't by a thrill.

I don't know whether to leave you,
or push you over the edge,
but still the pleasure is always mine,
no matter what I've said.

If you can't sit still,

you can't buy a thrill.

Something Wonderful

I'm crawling in my head with the walking dead,
I've got a cold sweat on my skin,
I'm fighting back the demons in a waking dream,
where my weakness will become a sin,
I'm holding onto terror, it's my guiding light,
it's gonna pull me out of my mind,
a never-ending telepathic testimony
to the fear that I feel inside.

Hell is not a place, it's a game you play,
and suffer every move you make,
possession is the prize in the enemy eyes,
you pay for every chance you take,
a soul is not a soul until it lives in a hole,
with a hacked-up life and limb,
the pain that you find can make you feel so fine,
the alienation's dead.

At the back of your mind,
go to the other side,
hello is anyone home?
but you've been left alone.

Maybe I'll submit to my own desire,
will the agony be too extreme?
something deep inside pulled my legs wide open
and the whisper turned into a scream,
took me by surprise when I heard my cries
because I didn't recognize my voice,
a schizophrenic call, or a voodoo doll,
too terrified to make that choice.

I've been stabbed in the back
by a maniac,
and I thought it was me,
but I didn't have the guts to believe.

Beyond good and evil lie the future ghosts
that surround us like a ring of flames,
summoned here by innocents and fools alike
for the pleasure of the game,
I wish to hell I was a stronger man
and I could heal just as quick as scar,
but I'm weak, when I'm in this deep,
it's not a game anymore, it's gone too far.

Creep

Nailed my soul to the bathroom wall,
kicking and screaming for a curtain call,
re-invented through a course of disease,
the germs decayed and then came back in threes.

Who's that scraping at the basement door?
Creepy crawl crying out "I want more."
Mama's little maniac throwing dice,
daddy's little diatribe, cold like ice.

How so? How's a creep to grow?
Heavens above! Now the creep's in love!
Strike three, creep pretends it's me,
backburn, where's a creep to turn?

Creep still playing with a fork and knife,
killing itself to lead a sheltered life,
murder and custom, and catholic guns,
mocking and useless to everyone.

You're sending out language to the dog in me,
locking my door like that so I can't breathe,
save me a taste of what you're biting back,
cut your religion out and paint it black.

Mr. Lucky

Mr. Lucky just hit the street,
and he's lookin' for something sweet,
he's gonna steal himself a cop car —
cheap ass blow, and a bite to eat,
"I'm gonna score me a B.P. vest,
pimp my intellect and burn the rest,
cut a few scars in the life story bar,
get a big load off my chest…"

"Don't you know I got two things on my mind,
first one's nothing, second's womankind,
introduce me to the fox with goldilocks,
and mama bear's behind—
a black cat's crossed your path,
Valentino and psychopath,
claw me in the light of the stars tonight
drown me in your bath…"

With her back against the record machine,
she's a 4 AM beauty queen,
if I throw a six, she's mine tonight,
underdressed and seventeen,
wait a minute—who's that lucky guy?
He's got the devil in his eye.
Rings on his fingers,
and an empty glass,
and a queen with a big surprise…

Mr. Lucky just hit the deck,
with the liquor in full effect,
lend me an ear, and a shot, and a beer,
and I'll pay with a third-party check.
Hey! What's the matter with you man?
You gonna burn me catch as catch can,
throw him a bone, and he'll leave you alone,
don't blink he's a lucky man...

Sergio

Wet/hate hands admitted,
and...
through dead nails,
all spitting sand...

Underneath it's strychnine
winds that change are never seen,
beasts that back to the wall and cry,
best of the hopeless never die.

For gods' sake forget to speak,
miles of what you've got to eat...

Terminal, the playgroup says,
off to the side with an average,
blaming the dolls like heretics,
apostles or inebriates.

Hold on tight,
we're going to wake,

Laugh to death
for pities sake,

Framed for crimes that never sold
lies and secrets never been told,
look just like the two of us,
standing at the terminus.

The Rockabye

Get your filthy hands off my ice cream,
put your filthy mind in my hands,
when you open your mouth, it's a smoke screen,
and nobody understands.

And I can see you through my window,
collecting dirt outside,
moving in circles with feathers and bones,
diseased and paralysed.

I licked my way to heaven,
I broke my arms for worse,
I want to go where fever flows,
and spiders go to church.

Barking up the wrong leg,
spitting at your friends,
your filthy hands forever stained,
the rockabye defends,

Do or die,
it's the rockabye,
roll on over,
mine tonight.

Butcher Flower's Woman

Butcher flower's woman,
she did what she could,
nothing beyond
what a good girl would,
did you take the bait?
Oh, woman, did you take that bait?

When you fell like the butchered

onto slabs wide open,
cut a fresh new life,
all that pale blue broken,
did you choke on your fist?
Oh, woman, did you choke on your fist?

I made an appointment,
do you want to take her,
don't call it by name;
B.U.T.C.H.E.R.
were you that impressed?
Oh, baby, that makes two of us.

Did you make an appointment?
Were you that impressed?
Did you take what you needed
and kill the rest?

You ought to take a leaf
out of Daddy's book,
all blood and petals
hanging from a meat hook,
'cos she who breathes last,
or not at all

hounding acrobats,
with sabre and tongs,
curse the bastards eyes
with a rag you stole,
from a bleeding butcher boy's
empty hole.

Bastard.

Dirt

Victims burn in the atmosphere
breaking our back to get down here
I turned a hand on a switch-off
don't try to run, keep your hands up
no one's better at doin' my worst
make me feel like dirt
you cross a line to the freak-show
how the hell was I to know.

Think who falls on of night-sticks
don't break nothing you can't fix
pull the body that hits my face
love is something you can't beat
someone circling someone's eye
pulled the wings off another fly
think you're handling two of us?
Just like you did it on purpose.

Everybody is faceless
stone cold and stateless
form a line to redemption
to re-increase the tension
grab a gun while they're still hot
well if you like it or not

dream a negative dream for me
just to handle the street.

At the Top

In between the lines
haunted by complexity
you know the hand that guides
cuts the nerve that feeds you

move in perfect time
to reach a point that isn't mine
anger grows, remains sublime
a total world that isn't mine
definitive and undefined
out of reach and faithless
satisfied in solitude

Stare straight ahead
stare straight ahead

Sinking teeth in sinking sand
forced a life into my hands
a long drawn out procedure
that makes me long for sanity

Ingenious to a fault
but fool enough to read my thoughts
fool enough to read my thoughts
fool enough to read my thoughts

I watched you with both my eyes
I touched you with both my hands
a long drawn out procedure
that makes me long for sanity

I would be so pleased
if I remained inflexible
rigid to a fault
where both my eyes stare straight ahead

Accept my inexperience
and learn to love my decadence
rigid to a fault
when both my eyes stare straight ahead

Stare straight ahead…

COCKSURE

Klusterfuck Kulture

Boom boom surprise and I gave you my answer
and you can't be a part of my culture
and I don't want to give you a lecture
fuckin' somebody else while you text her
your ride's been trashed and pissed on
and ya drive it without any clothes on
the space age Viking you are
too bad the rats that nest in your car
here we go:
all the fucked up culture aside
why the fuck d'you want us to hide
we're the ghost of a circus hung-over and worthless
desperate to kill like a Buffalo Bill
got a million on my back
all the bounty hunters whack
like commercials on TV
guess they see what I can't see
like a fuck buddy off of Craig's List
she's all hungover and worthless
tried to drop a dime that I'm a terrorist
so I sent her back to the circus boom boom surprise
and I gave you my answer
curator of klusterfuck culture
lap dance in lieu of the rapture

Klusterfuck kulture in the eyes of you motherfucker
klusterfuck kulture in the eyes of you motherfucker
klusterfuck kulture in the eyes of you motherfucker
motherfucker motherfucker motherfucker motherfucker
   motherfucker

Remember the time we went AWOL?
All fucked up on Seagrams and Nembutal?
Pissed in the Walgreens pharmacopia
real American dystopia
now a systematic surrender
me and Judas is out on a bender
setting fire to the klusterfuck kulture
not willing to heal the new fracture
electric character flaw
scraping all the wire 'til its raw
anti-social un-media
get fucked while I clone you and breed ya
oh your smartphone fell in the can
now you can only crawl where you ran
all your texts turned into a shit storm
don't wanna know where they came from
now you watch yourself get arrested
on a site that's over requested
ready to beg for your saviour
forgetting illegal behaviour

Remember the time on your birthday
drunk to the bone and still thirsty
breaking your wrists and your shoulders
trying to steal a service revolver
now the cops just use you to gamble
cos you set such a shitty example
bones broke like my royalty statement
there's a laugh track at my arraignment
hey remember that time after Christmas?
You're an afterthought on my wish list
currency like a new bride
from Russia with love and genocide boom boom surprise
and I gave you my answer
like Tina Turner I'm a private dancer

my culture comes alive like Frampton
you came home while I was pulling my pants on
I'm struck by a rock in a car park
and I'm running from the sun like it's near dark
am I the vehicle that you wanna be stealin?
The weapon you're so good at concealin'?
the mindfuck stuck in your head
the virus that spreads like your legs
and fuck you for sayin' you're entitled
with your face at the end of my rifle

Assault on Cocksure 13

A.S.S. ASSAULT!
A.S.S. ASSAULT!
A.S.S. ASSAULT!
A.S.S. ASSAULT!

Medevac lifted to my dealer's house
shakin' me with strip search eyes,
the brood on the rooftop
take their molotov masks off
and their bodies start to synchronize

The countdown characters and killswitch christs
off makin' millions on their own
the fantasy death squad
returning to play god
assault in the forbidden zone

I'm comin' in there
believe in me
my feelings and my mercy are leaving me
assault in semi darkness and certainty
before just being human gets the best of me

A.S.S. ASSAULT!
A.S.S. ASSAULT!
A.S.S. ASSAULT!
A.S.S. ASSAULT!

Literally livin' in the fallout world
resurrection wrapped around my neck
the deities and icons
all pulling their pants on
the sermon blackout full effect

Glass in every building breaks and bruises me
cuts me like the kiss of hell
the dead and the distant
alive in an instant
evaporating where they fell

Skeemy Gates

Artery is deadly
back before you met me
can't bleed in and you can't bleed out
'cos none of you will let me
a remedy won't mend it
your body heat don't send it
a lack of air ain't never fair
will artery defend it

Can't find the name of my muscle
just sent him out there to hustle
no fake IDs or mega disease
no pieces that fit in the puzzle
he's crawlin' from a bit of the past
and his action's broken the glass
a warped career withdrawal and fear

and his mercy's comin' home last

Artery don't friend me
back before you met me
can't bleed in and you can't bleed out
'cos none of you will let me
a remedy won't mend it,
your body heat don't send it
a lack of air ain't never fair
will artery defend it

Can't find the reason I'm herea dancefloor based on fear
think a cluster bomb's gonna keep you warm
if you keep your enemies near
now I'm lost like a cunt in a maze
it's the drugs or I'm going through a phase
like the engine died and I'm locked inside
maybe cheap but nobody pays

Skeemy gates!

Can't find the keys to my shack
burn it and I never look back
pissed on my papers and I won't see ya later
try to steal another ride but the engine's jacked
I'm lost like a cunt in the rain
my antique Gucci stained
rather than call I'm gonna just crawl
for a taste like a moth to the flame

You're never gonna grow to like me
but I'm hatin' on the way you spite me
the last thing I need is a violent breed
the last thing you want is to fight me
I'm talkin' from a force of habit

no pity, no I never did have it
I'll be first in line to commit my crime
no talking to the one who said it
now I'm slippy as oil on yr balls
I'm tryin' to get away from it all
I tumble and skate off the high skeemy gates
all the shit that I stole thru a hole in the wall
all my customers throwin' a shit fit
they're stickin' it to me like a misfit
I can pay it all back I can blow my stack
stand still when I'm coverin' distance

Skeemy gates!

Alpha Male Bling

I'M THE PRODUCT OF PORN
it's the reason I was born
when I look in the mirror
do you think I see a killer
do you think I even waver from revolting behaviour
I'm the christ at the end of a condom
in the u-bend
try to up the rate of my consumption—hourly
the negative effects of my prescription—shower me
makin' out with tranny's at the bus stop—sugar me
tryin' to block the number 'cos you must stop callin' me

The man who owns the most
you can suck it while I boast
you can watch me on TV
if you really don't believe me
read my fat lips—I'm a god and you're penniless
an A.T.M. goon with a rubber on my harpoon
tryin' to jack a car with my crutches—cripple me

tryin' to make a hooker in the Vatican—sit on me
tryin' to sign a statement at the cop shop—trippin' me
tryin' to flee the city so you won't try n' follow me

Shower me with lots of things
like money, drugs, alpha male bling
and when you've nothing left to spray,
then suck it turn around and pray
your pockets and your throat is deep
and everything you steal I keep
you can't run out of shit to bring
like money, drugs, alpha male bling
alpha male bling
alpha male bling
alpha male bling
alpha male bling

I'm a broke-down freak
with a rage that never sleeps
I'm your past destroyed
I'm a motionless void
I'm the finger on your mobile
strokin' pics til ya grovel
I'm your nemesis on Skype
like a blow job in a fist fight
tryin' to hide the evidence that no one will corroborate
you think this is a funeral
but everyone celebrates
a made for TV fuck-a-thon gets lost in transmission
the nakedness dissolving in a war of attrition

Shower me with lots of things
like money, drugs, alpha male bling
shower me with lots of things
like money, drugs, alpha male bling

when you've nothing left to spray
then suck it turn around and pray
your pockets and your throat is deep
and everything you steal I keep
it's not enough to make me care,
a wasted slut, a past it player
you can't run out of shit to bring
like money drugs alpha male bling
alpha male bling
alpha male bling
alpha male bling
alpha male bling

I'm a set of black holes
try to play conflicting roles
anaesthetic on my ass
while I'm diggin' out the broken glass
a word of advice
from my sedative paradise
shower me with scorn
from the moment I was born
tryin' not to hear the empty chants of sycophants
listen to me singin' and all you hear is dissonance
you like me 'cos I'm evil and I love you for your innocence
I'm sneakin' out the backdoor
while the cops collect my fingerprints

Guilt, Speed & Carbon

(Guilt speed and carbon)
a doctor holds you by your feet
(guilt speed and carbon) you break your neck down every street
(guilt speed and carbon) you broke the law and no one saw
(guilt speed and carbon) the game is still worth playing:
I don't know why you fly so low

you just can't wait to crash
your dirty hands and what they pray for
never came to pass

(Guilt speed and carbon) you cut the wire and spilled your gut
(guilt speed and carbon) the secret door discretely shuts
(guilt speed and carbon) an oil spill's metal shrieks and stares
(guilt speed and carbon) the white hot sting but no one cares

Trying to find a gap
ain't nothin' left open
so you're forced outta power
by the threat of miles per hour
crime over rhyme
you're a guilt trip in my timeline
solvent, hell bent
anywhere the money's spent
lookin' for a hole
in the street where you'll find me
suckin' on monoxide
mechanical and parasite
douche makes a joke
like a spear through your spokes
and you're tossed like a dog end
on a pool of accelerant

Guilt speed and carbon, guilt speed and carbon

(Guilt speed and carbon) building burning twice as hard
(guilt speed and carbon) reflected on your credit card
(guilt speed and carbon) an accidentally planned escape
(guilt speed and carbon) civilian outrage laid to waste

(Guilt speed and carbon) passed around like gutter disease
(guilt speed and carbon) looks faked on the surveillance tape

Tryin' to find a gap
tryin' to find a gap
tryin' to find a gap
tryin' to find a gap

Trying to find a gap
ain't nothin' left open
so you're forced outta power
by the threat of miles per hour
crime over rhyme
you're a guilt trip in my timeline
solvent, hell bent
anywhere the money's spent
lookin' for a hole
in the street where you'll find me
suckin' on monoxide
mechanical and parasite
douche makes a joke
like a spear through your spokes
and you're tossed like a dog end
on a pool of accelerant

Ah Don' Eat Meat, Bitch!

Beak beak beakity beak! Beak beak beakity beak!
Beak beak beakity beak!
Beak beak beakity beak!

Look what you found in your burger
look what you found in your fries
a beak from a mutant
or the tail of a dog
or a deep-fried pair of eyes

You're ordering off the menu

something that was dragged from the trash
burned and processed with a deathwish
American system cash
please may I take your order?
did I kill the one you want
it's a chance to repeat to the bovine elite
you were born such a useless cunt

Swastaco! Swastaco!
Beak beak beakity beak!
Use the hammer not the bolt
good enough to eat!!

Suck it dry, I dunno why
I don' eat meat bitch!
Slaughter slaughter everywhere!
I don' eat meat bitch!
Hook and pull, hook and pull
squeal beak beakity beak
they bump and grind but never mind
fence live electricity
draining blood straining blood graveyard factory
they persecute with boredom
de claw de beakity

One finger points at hook and pull
one finger points at murder
the savage itch of blood flow
is flowing so much further
I don't wanna judge what you stuff in yr face
but the way you do it is such a disgrace
and you suck on your bone
and you're left all alone
and your meat falls onto a spike every night
and the entrails decorate the wall with it all

and the animals shriek beak beakity beak

Cock Ripped to The Giddy Tits

Bushies and bennies in my Slurpee
Irish as a room full of Murphys
we're gonna fuck this town
turn blackouts brown
we're the sharks invading your party
let's bring the weekend in with a fist fight
stiff kicking and a five-finger goodnight
are you checkin' my bitch?
Do you think she's ugly?
No talking to me unless ya talk shite.

Frank Boothe crossbred with Rambo
sit still while I call you an ambo
you're the crawl, I'm the brawl
she's the blow-up doll
we're the guests that you just can't handle
in the can with your medicine cabinet
goin' thru it with a PDR dragnet
throwing up through a town
that was built to fall down
too staggering drunk to resist it

Drinkin' til my brain gets drop kicked
horny and I want to shoplift
thrown from bar from tap room to car
from forklift to amateur facelift
here come the ladies from planet bathtub
with speed and their barbed wire hand jobs
4 AM sex objects and malt liquor logic
at the Waffle House with all your clothes off

Silikon Suckaz

Money bags fall from Alkatraz walls uh huh
jack and black juice and a moment of truth uh huh
smoke from the media never gonna feed ya hah
silikon suckaz kneelin to the fuckaz uh huh
cleaned ina washing machine uh huh

Silikon suckaz pressed to the street
by their stuck down marchin' feet
they're drunk on someone's landfill
they're the shrapnel screen elite
with their solvent use and gun abuse
all that cash between their legs
they could pay for sex or surgery
while they give each other head

Silikon suckaz and I know it's a bust (I said)
but it's just the dog in me
they're stuck together by friction burnz
in a Ballard book fantasy
I said I know what it's like to be a creep on the move
between ambulance and porn
it's the luck of the draw for the pedestrians
and the pimps I'm trying to warn

Silikon suckaz and I know it's a must (I said)

Silikon suckaz slumped in clubland
with their shadows for company
credit's all bad while they quote de Sade
the disinterested up and leave
in a fit of survival they sucker their rivals
and escape by sleight of hand
the money's all trashed with cigarette ash

but the suckaz all understand

Drug-A-Bug

Drug a bug, ya don't heard it
tried so hard to avoid it
a laugh you can hear as it cuts to the middle
as you talk as you fear
and the laugh's all brittle,
is it safer to love?
is it safer to hide?
drug a bug lost in a landslide
all the cast in a car
as it crashed to the stars
all the bank and the cost
of a gasoline wash
drug a bug: don't hide it
ya don't need time to decide it
if you smash your brains on the dashboard—shame
and you tried so hard to avoid it
if ya smoke it up—cool
if you pump it up—old school
got a wire and it's fresh
it'll hang from your flesh
you'll be runnin' for a mile
in drug a bug style
all the rooms lined with foil
all the wires are wrapped in a coil
all the windows blocked
and the doors are locked
and the floors are slick with electric shock
got wheels then ya better start movin',
cos your enemy start to be cruisin'
all the logic flawed
with the mountain law

all the ethics and measures
and national treasures
if ya bump it up—sound
bad stash—unfound
and the message is lost
as it melts in the frost
and you snort your dreams to the ground
drug a bug don't hide it
don't need time to decide it
if ya throat gets slit by a dagger then shit:
and you tried so hard to avoid it

All the shit that you wear outside
all the daredevil shit that you ride
all the shit that you talk on the phone
all the shit that you Skype on home
all the porn that soaks in the tub
all the cash that you spend on drugs
all the places that you hid your blow
all the chicks that are never in the know
drug a bug just done fuck it up
Drug a bug, ya don't own me
you ain't got nothin' to show me
both hands in the air
once you've pulled out your hair
and surrendered cold
your maniac gold
the fists are fucking the air
the cops they just don't care
kids all trampled
soldiers amped
with drug a bug love to share

I'm starin' as you try to march
eyez and ya throat too parched

a corpse in the desert and seconds of pleasure
and you dried it back to the start
withdrawal? don't start
'cos I ain't got space in my heart
git powder and a place in my cigarette case
and an endless stream of remarks
drug a bug, don't hide it
don't need time to decide it
if your eyeballs roll then I feel for your soul
and you tried so hard to avoid it

All the shit that you call your own
all the shit that you've taken on loan
all the people that you try to blame
all the people that you call insane
all the shit that you dump in the sea
all the shit that you dump on me
all the faults that you can't correct
all the people that you disrespect
all the lives you've managed to wreck

Drug a bug just done fuck it updrug a bug maintain me
don't try and entertain me
just dump all your drugs
up a nose you can trust
and snort when you can't contain me
the truth's just fuckin' me up
drug a bug runs outta luck
the face just folds
once the jokes are told
and drug a bug's stare just stuck

TKO Mindfuck

I feel frustration
I feel the same
the way I'm distanced
is not to blame
dispose of safely
dispose at night
you can't risk seeing
what others might

I can't remember
the things I've done
like crawl to safety
when there is none
it's all a mindfuck
forensic faith
the doors and windows
won't keep it safe

Thrust in leave it in
first to die
TKO mindfuck TKO mindfuck
turn yourself in with a blackout lie
TKO mindfuck TKO mindfuck
blame it on the voice or blame it on the choice
TKO mindfuck TKO mindfuck
level of pain when the walls are stained
TKO mindfuck TKO mindfuck

I can't remember
the things I've done
like crawl to safety
when there is none

It's all a mindfuck
forensic faith
the doors and windows
won't keep it safe

Porno Drones

Gimmee gimmee gimmee to the porno dronez
shimmy shimmy shimmy to the porno drones

jackin' in the sky and you are never alone
never move a muscle on your porno throne

shavey shavey shavey for the porno drones
I'm teenage and I'm Russian for the porno drones
you give a little lovin' to the porno drones
another missile comin' with the porno drones
(ass to elbow ass to elbow)

It's the colour of the smoke in the sky
and all the things that you try
when you're gonna shoot a miracle
the wire structures hang like ruptured reports
from all the rifles you sport
I said it's gonna take a miracle
I'm raking razors with a porno disguise
it's every stroke I disguise
it's everything I find hysterical

Gimmee gimmee gimmee!

Gimmee gimmee gimmee to the porno dronez
shimmy shimmy shimmy to the porno drones
ya need a little sugar for the porno drones
I'm fuckin' Freddy Krueger for the porno drones

jackin' in the sky and you are never alone
never move a muscle on your porno throne
busted like a hooker with an NPR MILF
you stare up at the porno drones and talk to yourself
shavey shavey shavey for the porno drones
I'm teenage and I'm Russian for the porno drones

(ass to elbow ass to elbow)

It's the freakshow you were born to begin
like all the bullshit you spin
you're not afraid to be an animal
the drones cluster and move faster than light
I never said it was right
this porno fuel in porn terminals
a clean weapon and a social disease
take all the drugs that you need
the porno drones are invisible

Gimmee gimmee gimmee to the porno dronez
shimmy shimmy shimmy to the porno drones
ya need a little sugar for the porno drones
I'm fuckin' Freddy Krueger for the porno drones
jackin' in the sky and you are never alone
never move a muscle on your porno throne
busted like a hooker with an NPR MILF
you stare up at the porno drones and talk to yourself
shavey shavey shavey for the porno drones
I'm teenage and I'm Russian for the porno drones
you give a little lovin' to the porno drones
another missile comin' with the porno drones
(ass to elbow ass to elbow)

Severance Package

Don't need to touch me (oh you've got to be joking)
watch the voltage pass through me (goin' up in smoke)
just for leavin' a light on (you ain't got the power)
and you stalled on the highway (you've been waiting for hours)

You get special treatment (where you hiding the weapons?)
when you're kissing the pavement (where you learning your
    lessons?)
can't read your condition (are you playing the part)
can't tell you to listen (you were dead from the start)

I'm the guy you remember (I got all the answers)
I'm a corporate sting (taking no chances)
white collar boot boy (don't listen to me)
fascist boot thing (don't listen to me)

Burn it down together! I'm a corporate sting
Burn it down together! I'm a corporate sting

Check it: I'm a believer (you don't have to tell me)
a zodiac breather (goin' up in smoke)
a fist with a fan club (bleeding no more)
a five-knuckle fight club (blood on the floor)

Climbing up the buildings that you're burning down
the nemesis on premises but can't be found
see you later born traitor accident or plot
you must have slipped and plunged into the parking lot

A case of corruption (no paranoia)
a corporate sting (don't listen to me)
a case of corruption (no paranoia)
a corporate sting (don't listen to me)

Burn it down together! I'm a corporate sting
Burn it down together! I'm a corporate sting

Climbing up the buildings that you're burning down
the nemesis on premises but can't be found
see you later born traitor accident or plot
you must have slipped and plunged into the parking lot
I'm a corporate sting!
I'm a corporate sting!

Hustler Face

Marching down the back of your neck
when you got nowhere to go
I really think so
your prejudice is burned to my indifference
with nowhere to go
I really think so

All hail the twisted mind
that you can't ever leave behind
scaling fences made of metal bones
to penetrate forbidden zones
your god's alive and kickin'
sending signs remains indicative
of rusty nails through hands
in fast food brothels
neon rashes on this crippled shit
articulate the caustic action
flowing through your veins
you think you're higher?
well you're higher still,
and you can't pay the bill
oh the drugs! oh the pussy!
oh the things we do for luv!

learn your lesson: use your weapon
ain't it sweet when you're in luv

Polar nerves in hidden doorways
you're the one who hides the price
and you're prejudiced entirely
trying to liberate your vice
will you breathe when they walk past you
painting symbols on the doors
love's a void you owe your dealer
bleeding out across the floor
first in volume—last in manners
voices scramble—police scanners
think ya got me? nothing stops
electric heresy it's flowing from
my mouth like toxic water into
flame corrosive wine
think ya got me? well, ya got me!
I'm a symptom of the time

Marching down the back of your neck
when you got nowhere to go
I really think so
your prejudice is burned to my indifference
with nowhere to go
I really think so

Kollider Skope

Intense awareness that I'm careless
when I bust you out of jail
because you can't afford a private ward
I'm a diamond-studded slum lord

Streets are desperate, streets are cold

streets alive with plastic gold
you're droning—I'm zoning
you're foaming at the mouth

Don't got to call no ambulance
just listen to my dissonance
don't fuck around with arrogance
cos I'm the bitch that made you
don't mess the magic master plan
cos I'm the bitch that slays you
no lie: kollider skope incoming

Kollider scope incoming

Still flinching at the fear of defense
and I'm never gonna do it again
to die behind a secret sign
and I'm never gonna show you what's mine
no I'm never gonna give you the time

Inside a worthless share of hope
born to suck up all the smoke
it's easier to breathe it in
to choke it down and leave it in
kollider-insider
I'm deafer and I'm blinder
don't need to feel humanity
rejected from my history
don't fuck with my intention
it's the only thing that's real
don't collide it with my character
it's only made of steel
no lie: kollider skope incoming

Still flinching at the fear of defense

and I'm never gonna do it again
to die behind a secret sign
and I'm never gonna show you what's mine
no I'm never gonna give you the time

Kollider scope incoming
Kollider scope incoming

O.C.D. Got Game!

O.C.D. got game and it won't ever look the same
toilet soldiers in a toilet war
just freakin' cos they freak ya more
O.C.D. got TV too and carbonated spit
black horizon for your crime ring
and the state of mind to carry it

And I like it!
And I like it!

O.C.D. got game before it ever got a name
living lacerate the dying
long before I gave a flying fuck
O.C.D. believe me I'm not sitting still to get a thrill
I'm flicker stick meticulous and O.C.D. ridiculous

Times one for you/times one for me
times multiply got O.C.D. the minimal maniacal
minority got O.C.D. do you got shit you wanna hit?
Do you got time to sit on it?
Do you got shit you wanna see
just like your game got O.C.D.
And I like it!
And I like it!
And I like it!

And I like it!

O.C.D. you've got to breathe
you've got to stop don't let it bleed
that money's down your shirt and hit your goon squad
where it hurts
O.C.D. complicit but you blink ya might just miss it
a slave to my conditioning
but O.C.D.'s not listening

...and where am I now??
more than a headline
I'm trying to come down
an O.C.D. deadline and I like it it's a tight fit got me senseless...
    and defenceless!

Times one for you/times one for me
times multiply got O.C.D. the minimal maniacal
minority got O.C.D. do you got shit you wanna hit?
Do you got time to sit on it?
Do you got shit you wanna see
just like your game got O.C.D.

Cold Dick

Peel my face off a dash-cam
upside down on another man
ain't it nice to be free?
Anonymous fantasy?
Cops all robbin' you blind
nothing in your pockets, it's fine
but I feel you like a blade
bleeding and I'm also made
just like a gasoline martyr
nothing in the trunk to barter

currency collapsed like a cold dick
sweat with the stars like you're dopesick
killing's a character flaw
shouldn't be against the law
flames all lick at remains
scorched earth cleaning up stains

Oh you get to see it
and then you get to feel it
and you're never gonna have it
I tell you to forget it
you used to be anonymous
and now you're just afraid of us
I kick you out the picture just like a cold dick...
Now you get to feel it
I can't believe you feel it
you look just like you feel it
are you never gonna feel it
call me when you feel it
get ya story straight and feel it
you're never gonna never gonna feel it
Feel it! Show it! Steal it! Know it!

Timeline sent to the crime scene
lovin' up the corpse with a gangsta lean
ain't it hard when yr dead?
Blood then rigor instead?
Track marks over your heart
electric jump to start
and I got ya under my skin
waiting for the flies to get in

Feel it! Show it! Steal it! Know it!
Joke with a deadly punchline
black holes in your timeline

friction heat is electric
but it ain't gonna move your cold dick
killing's the reason we're here
other reasons disappear
god with a battery plan
adrenaline you're the man

Now you get to feel it
I can't believe you feel it
you look just like you feel it
are you never gonna feel it
call me when you feel it
get ya story straight and feel it
move it back when you conceal it
you're never gonna never gonna feel it
Feel it! Show it! Steal it! Know it!

Mighty Mouse

You can use my stash if you want it
you can play the TV when I'm on it
you can fill my bath full of Crisco
service all my komrades at the disco

You can climb a mountain made of hazardous waste
stick a flag on top that says "you're in the right place"
you can hack the Vatican and flood it with porn
but I think they got it covered when the curtains are drawn

Mighty mouse all big like a man
bored, and he just tore up the plan
recklessly considering theft
besides the fact I got nothing left

You can fry your brains with decisions

where to make the deadliest incisions
become a hired killer with a whisper
your own private army and enlister

You can't have failed to notice that
the room's filled with smoke
the powders in your inventory
are making you choke
you're close to acing all the tests that make you a douche
excommunicate/inebriate
I'm cutting you loose…

Mighty mouse all big like a man
bored, and he just tore up the plan
recklessly considering theft
besides the fact I got nothing left

Razor Invader

Razor invader, hope to see ya later
a minute too soon trapped inside a room
law is blaring loud circling the crowd
the circumstance is war developed at your door
reanimate your baby
you don't need to be careful
and I ain't gonna lie
I ain't gonna level
a message to ya mama
with a solar surprise
and I ain't gonna level
I ain't gonna lie

And I ain't gonna lie, I ain't gonna level
and I ain't gonna level, I ain't gonna lie
and I ain't gonna lie, I ain't gonna level

and I ain't gonna level, I ain't gonna lie

A dream of dissolution in a maze of condition
exploding like a dare, you never know it's there
infected blood ashtray runs away with your heart rate
your teeth on the floor, invader no more
circumstance is sorted, the plans have been aborted
you're never gonna feel, what's dangerous is real
a message to the missing/then separate the law
a world for you to steal
what's dangerous is real

A razor invader, a razor invader
bet you can't bend me round the eyes of a traitor
a razor invader, a razor invader
bet you can't push me past the bastard you are

And I ain't gonna lie, I ain't gona level
and I ain't gonna level, I ain't gonna lie

Razor invader, disease and instigator
you're crawling down the wall, you don't see me at all
fighting like a furnace, you never know the heat
you disengage direction, instigate infection
don't mean to sound insistent
you gotta keep your distance
don't wanna know you're there
don't wanna know you're scared
you might as well be murder
it takes you down much further
and you can raise your fists
no matter what the risks

A razor invader, a razor invader
bet you can't bend me round the eyes of a traitor

a razor invader, a razor invader
bet you can't push me past the bastard you are

And I ain't gonna lie, I ain't gona level
and I ain't gonna level, I ain't gonna lie

Hi Talez

Up to my neck and the last I checked
I was giving you a hand with the contraband
the SIM card soldiers sent to war
the dash-cam diaphragms keepin' up the score
what do you want from a drug like me
to be kicked in the nuts
as you try to be free
spray paint sacrifice is mine
you can follow the trail of spit to the crime
I'm the long lost bastard maniac man

Can't dance here with your homemade highs
tell your muscle to relax while everyone dies
with a speedball Saturday catch if you can
I'm a force of nature: hands on the mic
bathing in the vomit of the drinks that I spiked
I've become a loose cannon since I brought you down
crawlin' in the speaker just to hear the sound
number one like an overdose's greatest hit
but the money and the maniac are counterfeit

Down to the last of my chemical compounds
putting out feelers to the underground
hacking my woman on a burner phone
bug her for a sedative but nobody's home
I'm a score never settled when I'm on the mic
one hit wonder dying of fright

monochrome messiah at the cash exchange
jammin' with a cigarette and looking insane
security guard with piggy little eyes
rumpled and stained and paralyzed
can't smoke here but you can spread disease
neon yellow night club fantasies
I'm worse than a waste of time in flight
an urban sedative sacrifice!

Lager!
Lager!
Got 80 lakes of lager!
Got speed!
Got sex!
Got L.S.D. and cigarettes!

Get your high talez outta here!
Get your high talez outta here!
Get your high talez outta here!
Arriba! Arriba!

Get your high talez outta here!
Get your high talez outta here!
Arriba! Arriba!

Lager!
Lager!
Got 80 lakes of lager!
Got speed!
Got sex!
Got L.S.D. and cigarettes!

Heretic Hypocrite

Heretic hypocrite
dead at the core
laughing like a halfwit
then laughing no more
blunt force blistering
thoughts become smoke
heretic hypocrite
your god is a joke
heretic hypocrite
slumped in a crypt
praying like you're rabid
and your throat has been slit
life force lunacy
evaporate veins
heretic hypocrite
your god is insane

Bring on the angels!
No rapture no truth
lies lick like hellfire
we're looking for proof

Heretic hypocrite
flaunt your disease
coughing up a prayer
as you kill what you please
instant genocide
wipe out the worst
heretic hypocrite
your god is a curse
your god is a curse
your god is a curse
your god is a curse

your god is a curse

The Finisher

And you'll never get to take that trophy home
and you used it for an ashtray
you were waiting for a better day
your t-shirt stained 'cos it was never new
and it soaked through your chest
like you were lactating special brew

Finisher! Can't beat the finisher!
Finisher! You're just the finisher!
Finisher! God help the finisher!
Finisher! Here comes the finisher!

Here comes a waste of everyone's time
committed day drinker and to petty crime
a crudely formed lion on his tattooed neck
and "the finisher" scrawled by a drunk insect
majestic in the way he cracks his head
he should call for an ambulance but lights a cig instead
then he drones his endless story on the phone
lumbers through the saloon doors
and makes his way home

Here comes a stain on everyone's pants
he can empty out arenas with his pitiful stance
a tribe of mates who can't walk in straight lines
too drunk, too fucking stupid or just blind
a crossbreed of a cowboy and a slug
his pockets full of change
and unpredictable drugs
the framework of the lowest intellect
he walks blindly into traffic

just to see what he can get

He's a monster in the house
jive bunny crossed with mighty mouse
he's a hero on the scheme
lobbing bottles full of kerosene
he's the neighbourhood savant
acting like a total cunt

Teezer Hell

Rusted unreasoning
my legs weak from teasing
and the silhouette
the shape of middle fingers
too close to be atrocious
too cold to grant a dying wish
too washed up like a limb on teezer shores

And straight down the middle
undefeated force of will
using chemicals to dwell on teezer heartache
where smoke stretched up from urban freeze
condensing into weapons
raining loud they cut the cloud
of toxic metal

Make sure your blackened eyes
are side swiped by the irritants
a season of disease in teezer hell
you fall out of the guidelines
and you crawl out of parameters
you never want to leave this teezer hell

Most of this uncertainty

is brought here by deserters
ringing bells recoiling ashes coat the skin
fever failure from the wailing walls
that wake you into teezer hell
the air is still and weaponized to win
most of this conditioning
is teezer hell not listening
the forces dropping distance off a bridge
slice the branches off a dying tree
to burn yourself a history
infested with the things you never did

Yellow Dog

My master calls me the yellow dog
cower-must carnivorous
design defraud
to love you as a canine
in our purgatory
just gimmee back my sawblades
and my rivalry

Yellow dog-ripped from the tabloid innuendo
it's the only truth your claws can reach
spare the rod and spoil the child
of sunken journalism
yellow dog! you're just a yellow dog!

A post that you can lean on-just pissing in the wind
your territory marked with fucking trash
the yellow dog invades your face
with private sector combat
and waits for your devices all to crash

My children call me the yellow dog

in between the biting noises here is god
the soaking light serenity
is rabid now
public service antibodies
don't know how

My mind is fixed on the yellow dog
crawling under vehicles in a yellow fog
lowest form of caged employee lunges up
looking for another yellow dog to fuck

Baby, You, Me, and the Dark Web

Bitcoin! Bitcoin!

And I think I wanna travel
make the predator unravel
spending nothing in the fast lane
I gotta hack my baby's brain
you shout it like an insult
a cotton-robed death cult
throwing bitcoin at the saviour
combustible behaviour

Baby, you, me, and the dark web
I don't care what your mama said
we gotta surf it with your shades on
and our pants that got the stains on
baby, you, me, in a kill room
we'll just party 'cos we'll die soon
with a pocket full of bitcoin!
And the lives we are destroyin'

Bitcoin! Bitcoin!

And I put shit in a folder
nice to see the world grow colder
and I'll save it all for later
my apocalypse crater
and my taste is getting wider
oh my clinical decider
I'm a dark web or a death wish
just a path to resist

Bitcoin! Bitcoin!

Baby, you, me, and the dark web
gonna give us back our street cred
gonna get my credit card on
gonna swipe it with my hard on
baby, you me in a porn hub
vaping Ambien to Culture Club
a casino drenched in bitcoin
and the lives we are destroyin'

Bitcoin! Bitcoin!

Surgical Waste Repo Party

It's gonna take a while to drain this bile
because I can't find an antidote
it's like trying to run a race through this surgical waste
with a tube stuck down my throat,
the nurses and the bar backs turn around and ransack
the ambulance for broken devices
the punks and the docs do the Chinese rock
'cos you can't call a vice a crisis

I'm trying to keep the pace
with this surgical waste

in a repo party lost in a psych ward
the noise never stops
until your heart rate drops
and the doctor runs away with the drug lord

Happy day! Happy day! Surgical waste
The tubes they all came out to play
Anaesthetic anorexic day! Surgical waste
A medical emergency! Surgical waste

Liposuction!
Cell destruction!
Tract infection!
Face correction!

And everyone goes pale when the sirens wail
it ain't a party until there's blood loss
the dumping ground is sacred
amputations, bodies naked
bent syringes in the sign of the cross
patient zero is sincere when he
shouts "Let me back in here"
this is my biohazard heaven on earth
it's got these horror floors
that hosted everyone's wars
knee-deep in someone's afterbirth

Lotto Lout

10 BH is the number on the gate
and the readers wives redeemed
closed circuit pics
of anonymous dicks
taped to pictures of the queen
you made your home near some genetic car park

chain link vistas over dead-eye pigeon shit
alcopops and petrol bomb hysteria
panic dancing while your cigarette gets lit

Lotto lout
listen to the fuckwit shout
parrot fashion
world war ration
mugshot stained
with a tabloid frame
Herpes! Gout! He's a lotto lout!
Herpes! Gout! He's a lotto lout

We've got a winner!
He's a slobbering mess!
With his hands on his balls!
And a tattooed chest!
We got a winner!
She's a shoplifter!
Her name's Carlsberg Kate
failed grifter

Zero zero zero is the number of the room
in the hotel belligerente!!
Closed circuit comedy
a blow job while he's vomiting
suave!! intelligente!!
You built your family with fortune
a poundstretcher paradise
parading the prescription pantomime
xenophobic remedies
provincial extremities
the antisocial mudslide
that you climb

Sexy D.A.

There's nothing that can touch this
in the rotting halls of justice
I'm so sad to see the future go to waste
but she shimmies from her office
with a verdict in her hands
and there's blood upon the sexy D.A.'s face

I'm crawling from the crime design
I put the ass in asinine
perp walk upon the dance floor
slips and falls
now she's gliding past the DJ with Bacardi in her hands
just have an answer when the sexy D.A. calls

Make the evidence scream
when the hammer falls, sexy D.A.
I don't mind this legal streak at all!
Hidden loopholes and fat white assholes
gawk at her-sexy D.A.!
They try to grab her ankles as they crawl

In she walks with a sneer
and the jury is here
and they're hung like a stallion's dream
delivers with a voice a mysterious choice
and you don't know where she's been
cops outside
and the lawyers all hide
from the sexy D.A. death stare
delivered through the lens of her turncoat friends
and the snitches that she dares

My god you should have seen her

I drooled on my subpoena
I think I got a summons
I think I see it comin'

The closing speech seductive
and we were all seductive
the sexy D.A. told us
we just want her to hold us
my god you should have heard her
nothing would have scared her
the holding cells implored her
the legal team ignored her

Shockroach

Shockroach burning
pest, you're learning
stand your ground
and muscles flounder
drag your heels
synthetic clown
far too many legs
for just one gun
you can't hold back
you're loose in crowd
but you got no back
you're just a coward
to hang your ass
in shockroach shame
you turn around
and fuck the game
what makes your country great
is your own decay
you suck my blood
from miles away

dead antennae
someone's trigger
grab it tight
it makes you bigger

Here comes an army
nothing slows them down
fast weapons make 'em lighter
they don't need to be a fighter
just a shockroach shit contamination
in your fucked-up life emancipation
it's crawling through your home
it's kneeling by your bed
and it struggles through your head
to suck your blood again

Shockroach anger
sinks its fangs
into its fleshless
trigger finger
christ you're dumb
you think we're scum
your underbelly
shines oppression
spits aggression
in the garden
of your yes men
scum delivered
back in sections
as you monitor
the blood flow
and the volume
of the shock show
stick my fingers
in your sticky fascist eyes

you write your history
in hieroglyphic shockroach lies

Nothing but a shockroach

ACKNOLWEDGEMENTS

KIMBERLY BLESSING for decades of endless support, for making this book a reality and so many other projects as well, I will never be able to thank you enough;

SHIRLEY MANSON for your beautiful foreword and a lifelong friendship I cherish every day;

MICHAEL BEGG for such gorgeous cover art that gets absolutely to the heart of what I do;

MEGAN WALTERS for proofreading 40 years of work. Holy crap!

ALSO BY CHRIS CONNELLY

Confessions of the Highest Bidder

Ed Royal

Concrete, Bulletproof, Invisible and Fried:
My Life as a Revolting Cock

CPSIA information can be obtained
at www.ICGtesting.com
Printed in the USA
BVHW041949280320
576259BV00001B/1

9 780966 406573